THE
SUTTEES'CRY TO BRITAIN

THE
SUTTEES'CRY TO BRITAIN;

CONTAINING

EXTRACTS FROM ESSAYS PUBLISHED IN INDIA
AND PARLIAMENTARY PAPERS

ON THE

Burning of Hindoo Widows:

SHEWING THAT THE

Rite is not an Integral Part of the Religion of the Hindoos,

BUT

A HORRID CUSTOM,

OPPOSED TO THE INSTITUTES OF MENU, AND A VIOLATION of Every Principle of Justice and Humanity

BY J. PEGGS

GYAN

Published by

Gyan Publishing House
5, Ansari Road
Daryaganj, New Delhi-110002
Phone: 011-47034999, 9811692060
E-mail: books@gyanbooks.com

Distribution Network
gyanbooks.com
India, USA, Canada, UK, Australia

ISBN: 978-93-6433-230-9 (PB)
First Published, 1827

2nd Impression 2024

Printed at: Gyan Press, Delhi.

THE SUTTEES'CRY TO BRITAIN
Author: J. PEGGS

THE

SUTTEES' CRY TO BRITAIN;

CONTAINING

EXTRACTS FROM ESSAYS PUBLISHED IN INDIA
AND PARLIAMENTARY PAPERS
ON THE

Burning of Hindoo Widows:

SHEWING THAT THE

Rite is not an Integral Part of the Religion of the Hindoos,

BUT

A HORRID CUSTOM,

OPPOSED TO THE INSTITUTES OF MENU, AND A VIOLATION

Of every principle of Justice and Humanity:

RESPECTFULLY SUBMITTED TO THE CONSIDERATION OF ALL WHO ARE INTERESTED IN THE WELFARE OF

BRITISH INDIA;

AND SOLICITING THE INTERFERENCE OF THE BRITISH GOVERNMENT, AND OF THE HONOURABLE THE COURT OF DIRECTORS OF THE HONOURABLE EAST INDIA COMPANY, TO SUPPRESS THIS SUICIDAL PRACTICE.

BY J. PEGGS,

Late Missionary at Cuttack, Orissa.

"In childhood, must a female be dependent on her father; in youth, on her husband; *her lord being dead, on her sons;* if she have no sons, on the near kinsmen of her husband; if he left no kinsmen, on those of her father; if he have no paternal kinsmen, *on the Sovereign.*"

INST. OF MENU.

"The burning of widows is a mere excrescence from the corrupt stock of polytheism."

FRIEND OF INDIA.

London:

SEELY AND SON, FLEET-STREET; W. BAYNES AND SON, AND WIGHTMAN AND CRAMP, PATERNOSTER-ROW; WESTLEY, STATIONERS' COURT; BLANCHARD, CITY-ROAD: SOLD ALSO BY WILKINS, DERBY; BENNETT, NOTTINGHAM; NOBLE, BOSTON; AND ALL OTHER BOOKSELLERS.

1827.

THE

Suttees' Cry to Britain,

&c., &c.

SECTION I.

Remarks on the horrid nature of the practice of burning Hindoo Widows, and on the causes that tend to prevent its suppression or occasion its perpetration.

IT is a melancholy reflection, that the religion which influences the population of the vast regions of India, is totally unfavourable to the exercise of every principle either of humanity or virtue. Many of its precepts are so afflictive and unnatural, that they seem to have sunk by common consent into complete disuse; and if every point of the Hindoo ritual were literally enforced, not only would it be impossible to carry forward the ordinary business of life, but all those social relations, to which we are indebted for so much of our happiness, would be completely obliterated, and the whole frame of society dissolved. There are still, however, many usages subversive equally of benevolence and morality, which have been perpetuated for ages. Among these is the burning of widows, a practice, the enormity of which would strike even the Hindoos themselves, did not a blind attachment to the vices of their forefathers overcome every natural feeling. In all the annals of human depravity it will be difficult to discover a custom so horrible in its nature, or so destructive in its consequences both on individual and public happiness. It forms one of the blackest pages in the history of Hindooism; and were this feature of its character alone to remain on record, it would be of itself sufficient to hand it down to the execration of the latest ages. That a practice, which would reflect a stigma on the most barbarous tribes, should have been sanctioned by men of thought and penetration, and perpetuated among a people whose mildness of disposition is proverbial, shews to what a state of degradation the mind may be reduced under the influence of an unnatural superstition. This is not the case of a patriot relinquishing life to establish the freedom of his country,—it is not a martyr braving the flames to maintain the rights of conscience,—it is not a noble mind sacrificing even life itself on some occasion of exalted virtue to secure to posterity the benefit of its high example. On these occasions we feel a melancholy pleasure in applauding a voluntary resignation of life. But it is the helpless and disconsolate widow torn from her family at the very climax of her grief, and hurried to the flames amidst the shouts of an unfeeling multitude. She must stifle every feeling of compassion for the offspring of her womb, she must renounce them at a period when they stand most in need of her care; and, when weighed down with sorrow, she must take a last look on all mortal things, and enter the flames. Every feeling of humanity is here sacrificed, without the counterbalance of the least degree of advantage either to individuals or to society. Had this sacrifice been demanded of the stronger part of the community, even then it would have been a demand of singular enormity; but in a country like Hindoostan to demand this sacrifice of the weaker sex—to urge the unprotected female, while her grief for the loss which her children have recently sustained is yet unsupportable—to deprive them of their only remaining consolation, and cast them on the wide world, without a father or mother, is surely a case of unparalled barbarity, and tends almost beyond any thing else to develope the extent of the depravity to which Hindooism owes its origin.*

Were we to hear of a nation which, on her husband's death, subjected a widow to the loss of all her property, of which she might probably have brought him part as a dower which she had enjoyed with him from the time of their union; and turned her out on the wide world (her lord and protector being dead) to labour—to beg—to steal—or to perish, with what feelings of indignation should we regard such a law and such a nation! We should inquire, On what principle is this severity exercised on a helpless woman, precisely at the moment when her heart is torn with anguish through the loss of him on whom was fixed all her hope? Were *imprisonment for life* added to this outrage, however; were the hapless widow deprived of her liberty, as well as of all her property, the moment death had closed the eyes of her husband; such a procedure would excite horror and indignation in every mind. What then should we say were we to hear for the first time, that in some newly discovered island, the death of the husband sealed the doom of the wife, however virtuous and exemplary in her conduct; that she was, from that moment, devoted to death,—and to death in its most dreadful form—*to be burnt to ashes?* Such, however, is the case; not in some lately discovered island, hitherto totally cut off from the rest of mankind, but in India, famed for her literature and civilization; and, above all, in Bengal, where Europeans are chiefly found; whose ideas, the wise and candid among the natives are imbibing every day.

How then is it possible that the murder of the amiable and defenceless, attended too with such circumstances of cruelty, should

---

* Friend of India, (monthly series), Vol. i. pp. 301, 302.

have continued so long? How is it that common humanity has not overleaped every bound, and constrained superstition to desist from a course so barbarous and inhuman? Among other reasons which might be mentioned, this certainly has its share, that *the whole of the horrible deed is really concealed from view*. Had the deed been constantly perpetrated in the sight of all, as was formerly the case in Smithfield;—had the helpless victim to superstition been bound to the stake in the open view of the multitude, as were formerly the victims to Romish bigotry;—had the flames been suffered to kindle on her publicly;—had the convulsions and agonies of the widow expiring in torments, often in the bloom of youth, been fully witnessed by the aged, the young, the neighbour, the near relative, humanity must have spoken out long ago; reflection must have been awakened in the public mind. At least, parents and relatives must have felt horror while anticipating the agonies which awaited a daughter or a beloved sister, the moment sickness or even accident rendered her a widow; and the voice of nature must have prevailed, and abolished a practice so destructive in its anticipation to the peace of every relative, whose heart was not steeled against all the feelings of humanity.

But instead of this, the agonies of the dying victim *are completely concealed*, while her shrieks are drowned in the noise and shouts of the ignorant multitude and the unfeeling ministers of death; and thus the whole is as completely hidden from public view, as though the dreadful deed were perpetrated within the most secluded cloister. The concealment indeed is far more effectual; for in that case, though the shrieks might not assail the listening ear without, the imagination would unavoidably paint to itself the horrors of a daughter, a sister, or even an acquaintance, expiring in the flames, in a manner scarcely less vivid than the real view. But the victim's being thus brought before the multitude in a state which scarcely leaves her the power of reflection, her being hastily led through certain ceremonies, and hurried to the pile by those whose countenances wear the appearance of hilarity and cheerfulness, bound to the dead body of her husband, and covered instantly with the fuel, as well as *held down by a pressure which renders all resistance totally unavailing*, hides all the horrors of death from the sight; while the shouts of the unthinking crowd, which begin to rend the air the moment the torch is applied to the fatal pile, no less effectually conceal from the ear those agonizing shrieks, from which it is scarcely in nature to refrain at the touch of the flames. Thus completely are the multitude deluded: they think they witness all, while they witness nothing; and the unnatural jocularity, which, originating with the actors in this dreadful scene, generally pervades the whole crowd, removes every feeling of pity, and gives the whole rather the air of a joyous festival than of a funeral scene. The agonies, and shrieks, and dying groans, of the unhappy victim, are witnessed by no one,—but by Him who is the Avenger of blood. But are these agonies the less real on this account? Is the anguish of this tremendous death the less felt? Let reason and humanity judge.

Without entering into the origin and cause of this dreadful practice so deeply seated in the system of Hindooism itself, to do full justice to which would require a treatise instead of a short essay, we wish now merely to notice some of the most obvious circumstances which attend it. Among these let us consider for a moment who those are, who are doomed to undergo these agonies, unpitied, because never beheld. They are, *the most amiable part of the Hindoo race!* In most cases they are females possessing some degree of wealth, for the very poor seldom thus devote themselves to death: they are not worth the labour requisite to work up their minds to a sufficient pitch of delusion. If the term be applicable to any female in the present state of Hindoo society, they are in general persons of *education:* and whatever be the degree of polish and delicacy which accompany opulence, whatever the ideas included in a superior mode of living; they are in general possessed by those whom this dreadful custom marks for its victims. It follows, therefore, as a matter of course, that if among the higher ranks of society in this country there be any *delicacy of feeling*, it is possessed by these who may be said almost from their birth to be devoted to the flames.—And if there be any thing to be found of conjugal fidelity, it resides among these, since an extraordinary degree of conjugal affection, either real or ascribed, is made the lure by which these unhappy victims are betrayed to death; the enjoyment for numerous ages of the highest felicity with their deceased husbands, being held out as the bait to draw them on till they make the irrevocable declaration, that they will commit themselves to the flames. It is probable, therefore, that those who are thus cruelly murdered year by year, are in most instances the best educated, the most amiable, and the most virtuous, of the Hindoo race.*

If we turn from the wretched victim to the *unhappy offsprings* whom she abandons, what do we behold, but a sight of still deeper woe! —Scarcely recovered from the blow inflicted on them by the death of their father, they are hurried from their once peaceful home to the funeral pile, to witness the death of their mother! In other countries, the loss of paternal protection is, in some measure, compensated by the increased exertion of maternal kindness and solicitude: but under the influence of this system, their children are deprived of both parents in one day. A state of the deepest misery succeeds to a state of the highest happiness with such rapidity as almost to deprive them of the exercise of their mental faculties.—The family compact is destroyed with the suddenness of an earthquake. The corpse of the father is scarcely cold before their only living parent is bound to it, and consumed in their presence. But there are circumstances of still greater enormity attached to this system: The funeral pile must be lighted by the eldest son! Had this deed of darkness been consigned to some unconcerned spectator, to the brahmun who officiates on these occasions with such lively pleasure, or even to some distant and unaffected relative, this might have been some re-

* Friend of India, (mon. ser.) Vol. ii. page 319—322.

lief to the feelings; but it must be performed by the *eldest son*—the extinction of the hopes of the family is consigned to him. He accompanies his mother from his home to the banks of the Ganges, he stands by in all the agonies of grief during the performances of those tremendous rites by which she devotes herself to destruction, nor does he dare to lift an arm for her relief: he beholds his mother, endeared to him by the recollection of a thousand acts of kindness, thrown on the funeral pile like a beast of sacrifice, and *inhumanly bound* to the dead body of her husband with all those indications of brutal satisfaction which shed a tenfold horror on the scene; and surrounded by his weeping brothers and sisters, he lights up the pile which consumes the living parent with the dead, and extinguishes all their hopes of future tenderness and protection. Every circumstance which can aggravate this scene of woe is here combined; nor is it possible to conceive of any thing which could add a deeper tinge of barbarity that has been omitted.

If we would form an adequate idea however of the effects of this system on social happiness, we must not overlook *the state of prospective misery* which each family suffers long before the painful moment of separation arrives. The family in which it is known that the mother must, through the tyranny of custom, devote herself to the flames, is subjected for years to the most painful and afflictive anxiety. The happiness which they enjoy may be suddenly annihilated; a single day may reduce them from a high state of domestic felicity to the situation of the most wretched orphans. They feel that the death of the father will be only a signal for the more horrid death of their endeared mother. The anguish which such a state of suspense and anxiety must involve, may be more easily conceived than described. The longer they are indulged with the endearments of maternal affection, the longer is the state of misery prolonged, and the keener does that stroke become of which they are held in dreadful expectation: thus, that which under a milder institution is a source of joy, is here turned into an aggravation of expected wretchedness. The continuance of their social happiness is removed even from the common chance of mortality, and placed at the disposal of a merciless superstition; even the cup of bliss is mixed with the bitterest gall, and that season of life when, from the absence of care, the mind is disposed to the utmost gaiety and cheerfulness, is in many instances consumed in almost insupportable anxiety and distress.

The influence of this system is scarcely *less destructive to the general happiness of society.* It aggravates every natural calamity, and gives additional horror to every disease. In other countries the prevalence of an epidemic only serves to increase the energies of benevolence. In this country, however, there are no attempts made either to stem the current of disease, or to console the afflicted and bereaved. Those of the family whom the disease has spared, are only reserved for accumulated misery—the survivors, instead of receiving assistance, are cruelly deprived of that parent who could most effectually have afforded it. Every epidemic therefore assumes an aspect of ten-fold horror. This dreadful practice is not suspended during a period of general distress; in vain do the wretched offspring demand the life of their mother at a time, when from the universal prevalence of disease, her's is the only hand that can minister relief to them; this superstition is inexorable as death itself. When therefore the country is afflicted, as during the past year, with a destructive epidemic, the numerous victims to disease, the augmented number of female immolations, the number of relatives who tremble for their sisters or their daughters, added to the number of children who stand exposed by the ravages of superstition and death, to the loss of all parental aid or consolation, form a consummation of misery, to which no other country on earth presents a parallel.*

By whom this crime is perpetrated, is worthy of the strictest inquiry. With the victims themselves it can scarcely be said to originate; for, a few days previously, they are often as void of all desire to destroy themselves, as to destroy others; and they are generally averse to the deed till their minds are completely deluded by fallacious representations, and their heads turned with dreams of future happiness, impossible to be realized. But whatever delusion may reign in their minds, without the concurrence of the husband's relatives it would be perfectly harmless. The *deed is constantly encouraged by the relatives of the husband;* those of the wife on the contrary, being generally on the side for which nature pleads; although her own son, if old enough, *is obliged to kindle the pile prepared for his mother's destruction.* It is therefore on the husband's relatives that the fate of every female of respectability and opulence is suspended, however young she may be, the moment her husband dies: and when it is considered, that they are bound to her by none of the ties of consanguinity, it will not appear strange if some one or all of the following reasons should, in general, so preponderate, as to doom to the flames one for whom they can have little or no personal feeling.

The honour of the family. This is supposed to arise in proportion to the number of unhappy victims, who can be mentioned as having devoted themselves to the flames. The husband's relatives of course claim to themselves a certain degree of credit for having surmounted feelings of affection, which they never possessed, as they generally regard the poor unhappy relict with the same apathy with which they view a log of wood intended for fuel; while the number of widows in their families devoting themselves to the flames apparently from love to their husbands, gives rise to the idea that these relatives of theirs possess that excellence of character which rendered it impossible to survive their loss. That when the unhappy widow is regarded with the most perfect indifference, this alone should so weigh as to make them prefer her dying to her living, will create no surprise in those who are thoroughly acquainted with the native character.

The wish to get rid of a burden. A widow, though only twelve years of age, can never marry again. If her own relatives therefore be unwilling to support her, or not sufficiently opulent, she must live

* Friend of India, (mon. ser.) Vol. i. page 302—304.

with the surviving relatives of the husband to the end of her life. And although her life is far from being a plenteous and affluent one, yet a certain degree of expense is thus entailed on the family, and this possibly for a considerable number of years when she is left in the bloom of youth. The consideration of an expense therefore, though small, yet scarcely terminable within the space of their own lives, added to the trouble and vexation often arising from female relatives living together who can scarcely be expected to have any affection for each other, may possibly make them wish to rid themselves at once of a heavy burden, when it can be done in a way which, instead of being esteemed dishonourable, or any proof of the want of affection, on the contrary reflects a high degree of lustre on the character of the family. At least this is a temptation which humanity would not throw in the way of a Hindoo who sets so little value on human life.

This is heightened by another consideration. It has been just observed, that *these widows, however young, can never marry again.* Now while impurity reigns among these very relatives of the husband, perhaps in such a degree as to attach to itself no kind of disgrace, a deviation from purity of conduct in a widow, would, in the public estimation, fix an indelible stain on the family of the deceased husband. When therefore the hazard of this dishonour through perhaps a long life, is present to minds, in which no natural affection towards a brother's widow is supposed to exist, it will excite little surprise that men who, (if report may be credited), in some instances make no scruple of hewing in pieces a wife of their own on a mere suspicion of inconstancy, should, on the death of her husband, decide also on the death of his unhappy relict, who, should she live, instead of contributing to the support or the honour of the family, would entail on it a constant burden of expense, and might possibly involve it in disgrace, when her death, while it frees them from all expense and anxiety, tends to heighten in no inconsiderable degree its general reputation.

To this may be added another circumstance which humanity will still more strongly regret. The *death of the mother deprives her children of their natural guardian*, their tenderest, most faithful and watchful friend, who can never see them injured with apathy, and who is ready to hazard life itself for the sake of preserving to them what is their own. It sometimes happens that a man who is opulent, dies and leaves children in a state of mere infancy. That their wealth should never be desired by the surviving relatives, is what no one will expect who is acquainted with the history of human nature, and much less those who are aware with what earnestness one brother among the Hindoos, will labour to supplant another even while living. That, in cases of infancy an affectionate mother, whom no cunning can elude, and no sum can bribe, should stand in the way of the surviving relatives of her husband, is only what might be naturally expected. Were she removed, there would be no one, at least with *her* feelings, to call them to account for the expenditure of the yearly revenue of these helpless orphans; nor possibly for the dilapidation of their whole property. The history of orphans, even in Christian countries, sufficiently shews us, how dangerous in the hands of presumptive heirs, would be such a power of removing, under a religious pretence, the mother of rich but helpless orphans. All these therefore, are so many temptations to the destruction of a widow, which through this dreadful practice, may be accomplished without the least suspicion being excited of the real views of those interested in her death; and were these suspected, still without that public virtue being excited in the country which would urge any one to step forward and save the widow from death, and the orphans from oppression and poverty. Whoever considers all these circumstances, and reflects that a mother may thus abandon, to the mercy of those who are presumptive heirs to all his possessions, however great, *an infant son only two years old*, will cease to wonder that so many widows are encouraged to destroy themselves; particularly as this dreadful practice is not confined to brahmuns, but extends itself to the writer cast, and even as low as to those who practise the trade of a barber!

Whatever be the delusive ideas which may apparently urge a widow to self-destruction, as the hope of her enjoying numerous ages of felicity in company with her husband;—of expiating the offences of her late husband and his ancestors, and those of both her father and mother's race, with other things of this nature, there are other considerations which cannot but come still nearer to the mind of the unhappy widow. She cannot but be aware, that those who have encouraged her in these fond hopes, are either those in whose power she is completely for the rest of her life, or such as are intimate with them; for although the husband's relatives affect to dissuade her from the deed, it cannot be difficult to discern which way their minds really lean. From these then, even the slightest hint, *that they wish her to die*, must operate on a widow of delicacy and sensibility, like a sentence of death pronounced by a judge. With what feelings could she commit herself for life to the mercy of those who had discovered this wish in the slightest degree, and felt in the least disappointed by her refusing to precipitate herself into the flames, particularly when the laws of the country provide her so little relief against any unkindness or barbarity she might hereafter experience from them? The law itself indeed insists that, while she is never to marry again, she is also to lay aside every thing like ornament for the rest of her days, and every sign of cheerfulness; that she is never to make a full meal, and that one day in every week she is to devote wholly to fasting and grief to the end of life. In these circumstances it is almost impossible that any degree of ill-treatment which the resentment of her husband's relatives might dispose them to inflict on her, could interest her neighbours in her sufferings so as to procure her redress; particularly when the interior of a Hindoo habitation, surrounded as it often is with walls, is nearly as impervious as an ancient castle, and the female relatives are scarcely more in the public view, than were formerly the unhappy inmates of its dungeons. In these circumstances, therefore, it is not strange, if, at the most distant intimation of this nature from those on whose kindness depends every future mitigation of her lot, and this prospect before her in case of a refusal, a widow of sensibility and reflection should feel almost distracted, and prefer a speedy death to the unknown horrors of her future destiny.

There is also another fact which ought not to be overlooked. Certain brahmuns perform the ceremonies observed at the funeral pile on which a widow sacrifices herself. These brahmuns receive even from the most indigent families something on a widow's actually devoting herself to the flames; and from some wealthy families as much as *two hundred rupees on these occasions.* While, then, it is the obvious interest of these brahmuns that the wife should be induced to destroy herself when the husband dies, they have access to every family, and are acquainted with the age and circumstances of the various inhabitants, especially of those who are wealthy. That they should constantly recommend this dreadful practice, and prepare the female mind for the perpetration of the deed, particularly in cases where the husband is aged or sickly, is the natural effect of their caring for their own support. But these brahmuns, as they are in some cases the family priests, are in habits of familiar acquaintance with the husband's relatives, and have much to expect from them. In what dreadful circumstances then must a helpless female stand, who has for her spiritual adviser on the subject of her living or dying, a man who has every kindness to expect from those who are presumptive heirs to the property of her infant son, or who may merely dread her devolving on them as a burden to the end of life! Nor is it necessary to suppose that brahmuns in forwarding the views of an infirm husband's relatives, and preparing the mind of the wife for self-destruction, should consider themselves as actual auxiliaries in the murder of a fellow-creature. They of course must be supposed to be as much habituated to the employment, from which they derive their gain, as a slave-captain formerly was to kidnapping and selling slaves, of whom probably a third died in the middle passage through ill treatment and want of air. They may possibly regard the act as meritorious, rather than cruel, and admire those relatives who thus wish to raise the reputation of their families, through the death of their brother's widow. And in this case even the distant prospect of a large remuneration, may urge them so to work on the mind of a simple, artless female, whose age is perhaps under twenty, that at the moment of the husband's death, no persuasions shall be needed to induce her to make the fatal declaration—beyond the *insiduous dissuasions* of her husband's relatives, increasing her desire by affectedly doubting her resolution, and really inflaming her vanity. Were these relatives, however, sincere in these dissuasions, they have it always in their power to prevent the act, as both the preparation of the funeral pile, and all the cost and expenses of the widow's destruction, devolve wholly on them, without the exception of the fee to the brahmun who thus assists in the actual murder of the young, the amiable, and the defenceless.

That other feelings than those of unconquerable affection for a husband, often twice or thrice their own age, or than any inspired by a steady belief in those wonderful tales of conjugal felicity to be enjoyed with him for boundless ages, influence the minds of the greater part of these unhappy victims, might be shewn by numerous instances wherein widows have been prevented by accident from burning.—Of this kind is an instance which occurred a few months ago, in a village about four miles from Serampore.

A man of the writer cast, at Kona-*nugura*, about four miles south of Serampore, between twenty and thirty years of age, died in December last, leaving two wives, one about thirteen years of age and the other about sixteen. Both of these, in the usual manner, expressed their wish to burn themselves with their deceased husband. The eldest of them being pregnant, however, was advised to delay till after her confinement, and then to burn herself with something belonging to her husband. The youngest, not being prevented, was burned with the corpse, of her husband. The eldest solemnly engaged to burn herself a month after her confinement; till which period she was taken home by her own parents. She at first expressed such displeasure at being thus denied the opportunity of burning herself, as to beat herself severely and possibly accelerate the time of her confinement; but, at the expiration of the month after that period, when called upon to fulfil her engagement, she had considered the subject more at leisure, and being at home in the house of her own parents, she positively refused to destroy herself; nor could all the appeals made to her feelings, all the threats and reproaches poured upon her, alter her resolution in the least degree. She was in the house of her parents, and completely independent of her husband's relatives; and as every thing which could be done was of course confined to verbal exertion, she determined to remain with her parents, where she continues till this day.

As this instance is by no means a solitary one, we have little reason to conclude that the desire to destroy themselves is more firmly fixed in the minds of multitudes besides, than it was in the mind of this young woman: the apparent wish to die which is thus factitiously produced, is in most instances the mere effect of circumstances created by others; and therefore no more exculpatory of the guilt of deliberate murder, than would be a man's intoxicating another with wine, or any deleterious drug, so as to deprive him of the power of resistance, that he might secure his destruction. Such then are the circumstances in which the most amiable and virtuous among the Hindoo women are constantly placed; circumstances are already hinted, by no means confined to the sacred tribe, but extended to the lowest casts among the Hindoos, as often as there is credulity enough to render the delusion sufficiently strong to become fatal.

If these circumstances be carefully weighed, it will appear that this inhuman practice has not even those pretensions to its being *a religious ceremony*, which most people have been ready to imagine. That it has *no foundation in any peculiar command given in the shastras* we have already had occasion to shew in our strictures on that valuable tract on the subject ascribed to Ram*a*-moh*una*-ray*a*, which was reviewed in a former number. Nor indeed is there in the ceremony itself any thing that marks it as being peculiarly of a religious nature.

The woman devotes herself to no deity; her professed object is merely that of rejoining her husband in a state of happiness. It is true that certain brahmuns officiate and obtain a sum of money on the occasion. But this is not peculiar to this ceremony: in almost every concern of life brahmuns are called in, and there are few which are not to them a source of profit.

Nor is this practice by any means prevalent in other parts of Hindoostan in the degree in which it now exists in Bengal. Of this the following letter contains a proof, which was sent us on the subject some months ago, by a gentleman who has been some years resident in Hindoostan.—

"I cannot forbear expressing my pleasure at seeing that the Editors of the 'Friend of India' have taken up the cause of humanity in calling the attention of Government and of the public towards the abolishment of Suttees. People in Bengal are not generally aware how unfrequent is this most barbarous custom in the upper provinces of Hindoostan. In eight years, mostly spent in this quarter, no Suttee has come to my knowledge; and my moonshee (a kshu*triya*), a man of about forty-five, informs me that he never saw but one, and that was at Lucknow; the victim, a widow of a Cashmerian pundit. There can be no doubt but a law of prevention would neither create surprise nor resistance in these provinces, and were it enacted for them only, it would lead to its being established hereafter in Bengal, should the Government hesitate as to the propriety of making it more general at present. Feeling you have done little towards a more glorious work until the minds of the natives be prepared by some change from their present insensibility and cruelty, I have written more at length than I intended, and beg your excuse for it."

This letter furnishes a pretty strong proof, that the cruel practice has in it more of the nature of a civil, than a religious ceremony. It is a well-known fact, that in Bengal, at the present time, the Hindoos are far less tenacious of their religious tenets and ceremonies than in almost any other part of India; that they are far less careful respecting caste, and that the brahmuns in numerous instances are guilty of actions which, according to the strictness of the law respecting caste, would degrade them completely. We have heard it mentioned as the opinion of Hindoos well acquainted with the subject, that were the law of caste enforced in all its strictness, there would be few families around who would be wholly safe. Yet the number of widows who are thus put to death scarcely at all decreases. It seems indeed to increase in the vicinity of the metropolis, where the greatest laxness is to be witnessed relative to things wholly religious. How can we account for this vast disparity in the number of these murders perpetrated in Hindoostan, and in the lower parts of Bengal, without having recource to other motives than those of a religious nature? But the moment we recur to *other* reasons for the continuation of this murderous custom, they present themselves on every side. The want of feeling manifested by the natives to their own countrymen when in danger of death by accident, as in a storm, or even when actually drowning, is known to most Europeans. The venality with which they are charged relative to oaths, is not without foundation; yet these must often involve life itself, as well as character and property. That they should then be peculiarly tender of the life of a brother's widow, who must at the best be a burden on them to the end of life, and who *may* bring disgrace on the family, is a thing scarcely to be expected. And when we consider the circumstances in which the widow is placed, together with that want of regard for human life, which is both the effect of their religious system and the characteristic of the nation, instead of being surprised that so many widows are every year cruelly destroyed, we shall rather wonder that any escape these fatal lures, when the husband's relatives so evidently encourage the practice.

Such then is the real state of the case respecting the burning of widows, which so many have been almost ready to tolerate under the idea of its being a most sacred religious ceremony, with which it would be sacrilege to interfere. With almost as much justice might the Slave Trade have been regarded with veneration, as a sacred relict of antiquity handed down from the earliest ages;—or the practice of killing all prisoners taken in war;—or that of sacrificing hecatombs of men at the funeral of a favourite chief;—or the conduct of certain banditti in this country, who, (from time immemorial no doubt) are said to seize men and immolate them at the shrine of their imagined deity. *It has scarcely enough of religious ceremony connected with it to varnish it over with the name of religion.* It is generally accompanied with the most unfeeling jocularity. Instead of its being a deed of mere superstition, there is reason to fear that it is too often the offspring of the meanest self-interest. It has not even the features of religion. *It is not binding on all.* It falls only on one sex, while the deed is perpetrated by the other, whom it can never reach; and of that sex it affects only one description of persons, and with these it is professedly optional: were it a religious ceremony however, it would be binding on all. But this class, while generally the most amiable and virtuous, are the most defenceless,—are left as fully in the power of relatives who do not *profess* any feeling for them, as the kid when in the paw of the tiger. It is never equally the interest of the husband's relatives that the widow should live, as that she should be burnt to death. With the former there is connected in *every case*, a certain loss of reputation, and the expenses of maintaining a person to the end of life in whose welfare they feel no kind of interest; with the latter, the full removal of this burden, and a high degree of reputation to their families.

So much do these circumstances affect the case, that were second marriages esteemed honourable, and the children born of them permitted to inherit equally with those of a first marriage, a practice sanctioned not merely by the laws of all Christian nations, but even those of Greece and Rome notwithstanding their idolatry, many think, that this alone would gradually extinguish the practice. But is it right, that in a country so richly endowed with the bounties of Providence, the mere question of interest, the loss of a few rupees annually, should be suffered to doom the most amiable, the most virtuous of our Hindoo subjects, almost daily to the most cruel death in nature; merely because their being uninformed in mind renders them liable to the grossest deceptions, and their being unable to support themselves, renders them dependent? We would intreat all our readers to remember, that *murder concealed from public view is murder still;* and, that our not actually witnessing the dreadful deed, when we are certain that it is committed, will do little towards exonerating us from guilt.*

SECTION II.

The cruel rite of Suttee not enjoined by the most authoritative of the Hindoo Legislators and opposed to their views of eminent virtue. Force absolutely forbidden by the Shastras, yet generally employed.

A learned native, already well known among our countrymen by his luminous examination of the Hindoo theology and philosophy, has printed and widely circulated a tract in the Bengalee language, the object of which is to dissuade his countrymen from the practice of these horrid rites; and has likewise published a translation of the tract in English. The tract is in the form of a dialogue between an advocate and an opponent of the system. The advocate cites various passages from *U*ngira, Vyas, Hareet, and the R*i*g-ved*a*, which enjoin or applaud the practice of self-immolation. Against these passages the opponent produces an extract from M*u*noo, the great Hindoo legislator, of whom the Ved*a* itself says, that "Whatever M*u*noo has said is wholesome;" which Vr*i*h*u*sp*u*ti corroborates by adding, "Whatever is contrary to the law of M*u*noo is not commendable." The extract is as follows: "Let a widow emaciate her body, by living voluntarily on pure flowers, roots, and fruits, but let her not, when her lord is deceased, even pronounce the name of another man. Let her continue till death, forgiving all injuries, performing harsh duties, avoiding every sensual pleasure, and cheerfully practising the incomparable rules of virtue which have been followed by such women as were devoted to one only husband."

From this passage the opponent infers, that as M*u*noo directs the widow, after the death of her husband, to pass her whole life as an ascetic, he intended she should *remain alive* for this purpose; and hence that this direction of M*u*noo is totally opposed to the directions of the other sages; and that their authority must bend to that of this great legislator. The opponent then adduces, as his next argument, the disesteem in which the generality of the Hindoo sages regard works of merit or demerit, or more properly, works done with the interested motive of gaining future happiness thereby; and to shew that these are not necessary to the attainment of what the Hindoos esteem the highest state of felicity, absorption in Brumhu, he quotes the following passage from the Ved*a*: "By living in the practice of re-

* Friend of India, (mon. ser.) Vol. ii. Page 322—332.

gular and occasional duties, the mind may be purified. Thereafter by hearing, reflecting, and constantly meditating on the Supreme Being, absorption in Brumhu may be attained. Therefore, from a desire during life of future fruition, life ought not to be destroyed." The immolation of the widow being urged on her wholly on interested motives, that of enjoying numerous ages of happiness with her deceased husband as its fruit, is therefore opposed to that system, which, disregarding all actions connected with bodily enjoyment, magnifies the value of divine knowledge as leading to absorption in Brumhu.

The advocate for the practice replies to this; that the later authorities, in directing a woman to burn herself, do not contradict this law of M*u*noo; and supports this idea by saying that M*u*noo directs the performance of Sundhya or evening worship, but is silent as to worshipping Huri, by calling aloud on his name, while Vyas prescribes calling on the name of Huri, and adds that the words of Vyas do not contradict those of M*u*noo. He therefore infers, that when V*ishnoo* and others command the widow to follow her husband through the flames, they do not contradict the command of M*u*noo. This the opponent meets with the utmost ease by shewing that there is no analogy in the cases, the performance of Sundhya not preventing any one's invoking the name of Huri during another part of the day, while a woman's burning herself with her husband will infallibly prevent her living the life of an ascetic; and completely fixes the charge of contradicting the immutable laws of M*u*noo on those who have prescribed this practice, by quoting *U*ngira as declaring that there is no other way known for a virtuous woman except her ascending the funeral pile of her husband; and Hareet as denouncing her refusal as a crime by declaring, that as long as a woman *shall not* burn herself alive after the death of her husband, she shall be subject to transmigration in a female form. The advocate for the practice endeavours to justify it farther by quoting the R*ig*-Ved*a* and Hareet, as commending it. This the opponent bears down by various passages esteemed sacred by the Hindoos, which reprobate men's performing religious rites merely from interested motives, and among the rest the following from the Bhagvut-Geeta, which he terms the essence of all the Smritees, Poorans, and Itahases, "All those ignorant persons who attach themselves to the words of the Ved*as* that convey promises of fruition, consider those falsely alluring passages as leading to real happiness, and say that besides them there is no other reality. Agitated in their minds by these desires, they believe the abodes of the celestial gods to be the chief object; and they devote themselves to those texts which treat of ceremonies and their fruits, and entice by promises of enjoyment. Such people can have no real confidence in the Supreme Being." These passages the advocate at length acknowledges to be indeed consistent with the Ved*as*, with M*u*noo, and with the Bhagvut-Geeta, adding however, "But from this I fear that the passages of the Ved*as* and other shastras, that prescribe Concremation and Postcremation as the means of attaining heavenly enjoyments, must be considered as *only means to deceive*." This the opponent of the practice very dexterously obviates, by urging that these could intend no deception: they only set before mankind *two* methods of obtaining happiness, the one excellent, the other mean and unworthy for those who are enveloped in desire, passion, and cupidity, who, if they had no shastras holding out rewards, would reject all shastras, and follow their own inclinations like an elephant unguided by the hook. To prevent this the shastra prescribes various ceremonies, among which is one for procuring the destruction of an enemy! and of course this for destroying widows.

Unable to urge any thing better, its advocate insists, that after all, a practice handed down to them by Hareet and others ought not to be set aside. This his opponent meets not only by saying that this argument is inconsistent with justice, but by urging the violation of their own rule in the very act of burning. The direction is, that "the widow shall voluntarily quit life ascending *the flaming pile* of her husband." Now, says he, "You first bind down the widow along with the corpse of her husband, and then heap over her such a quantity of wood that she cannot rise. At the time too of setting fire to the pile, you press her down with large bamboos. In what passage of Hareet or the rest do you find authority for thus binding the woman according to your practice? This is in fact deliberate female murder." The advocate urges as an excuse for this horrid practice, that were the woman to shrink back terrified with the flames, after having recited the usual incantations, it would be sinful, and be considered disgraceful by others. The sin his opponent treats with due contempt, by saying that according to themselves it could be expiated by bestowing the value of three kahuns of cowries, or twelve annas; and justly reprobates the idea of esteeming the prevention of murder a disgrace. The advocate for the practice, driven to his last resort, defends the binding down of the afflicted widow merely on the ground of its being a custom observed throughout Hindoostan. This his opponent first denies, and then justly reprobates, even were it thus universal. On this part of the subject we think it right to add a word or two.

In the burning of widows as practised at present in some parts of Hindoostan, however voluntary the widow may have been in her determination, force is employed in the act of immolation. After she has circumambulated and ascended the pile several natives leap on it, and, pressing her down on the wood, bind her with two or three ropes to the corpse of her husband, and instantly throw over the two bodies, thus bound to each other, several large bamboos, which being firmly fixed to the ground on both sides of the pile, prevent the possibility of her extricating herself when the flames reach her. Logs of wood are also thrown on the pile, which is then in flames in an instant; for to such a pitch of cruel ingenuity have the brahmuns, accustomed to officiate on these occasions, attained by frequent use, that the whole of this process is realized almost with the rapidity of thought. Scarcely a single moment is left to the spectator to contemplate the scene before the unhappy woman is writhing in the agonies of death. The author of the pamphlet under review states, that this practice has been recently introduced, and that it is confined almost exclusively to Bengal. This information, we have reason to believe, is perfectly correct. A few months ago, in one of the largest cities in Hindoostan, a woman who had devoted herself to death, and had even ascended the funeral pile, leaped out of the flames, and plunged herself into the river. Her relatives seized on her, and dragged her back to the pile; but she uttered the loudest cries, calling upon the officers of justice who attended to save her from a forcible death. They instantly interposed their authority, and on finding that she stedfastly resisted the wishes of her relatives, ordered her to return home; and though this scene occurred in a large city highly bigoted to Hindooism, and in the presence of thousands of spectators, there was not the least attempt made to rescue her from the protection of the officers of Government.

Before the late regulations of Government restricting the practice to the cases permitted in the shastras, many instances occurred of young widows, who, having refused to burn after approaching the flames, were forcibly thrown on the pile by their unfeeling relatives, that they might avoid the disgrace attached to a failure in such cases.

The use of force by means of bamboos is, we believe, universal through Bengal; it is intended to prevent the possibility of the widow's escape from the flames, as such an act would be thought to reflect indelible disgrace on the family. The number of widows burnt in Bengal, however, exceeds, by nearly three times, the number burnt in all the other provinces of Hindoostan besides. Thus in three cases out of four that force is used which renders all resistance on the part of the unhappy sufferer vain. This is totally contrary to the rules even of those shastras which command the practice; they strictly enjoin that the sacrifice shall be perfectly voluntary in every stage of its progress. Constraint indeed is forbidden by the very nature of the sacrifice. It is called a Suttee, because a woman devotes herself to the flames to prove that she has continued immoveably faithful to her husband. Not only therefore must the intention be voluntary, but to evince this, the act of immolation must not include the most distant idea of constraint. The use of bamboos is therefore at variance with the nature of the sacrifice, and with all the rules by which it is supported, and which direct, that she shall not ascend the pile before the flames are kindled. It is the *flaming pile* of her husband, that she is enjoined to ascend: and the immense difference between ascending the *flaming* pile, and being bound firmly down before the flames are kindled, must be obvious to all.

The Supreme Government has now for several years issued various regulations to the Magistrates, strictly forbidding the immolation of widows in cases where the Hindoo shastras have forbidden it; and surely if "a vigour beyond the laws," be ever tolerated, it should not be when the law has originated in the most savage barbarity, and is held doubtful by the wisest and most virtuous among the Hindoos themselves*—when its operation is levelled, not against the ruffian who eludes justice, but against the most amiable and helpless part of

* Mritunjoy, the head pundit of the Supreme Court, has given it as his opinion, that Brumhacharya, or a life of mortification, is *the law* for a widow; and that burning with

our Indian fellow-subjects. Under the influence of the former regulations many females of tender age have been rescued from destruction, yet not a single murmur has been heard throughout the country; no one attempt to counteract the wise and benign intentions of Government, or to employ force in the cause of inhumanity. Were the use of bamboos forbidden also, and the horrid sacrifice made to assume the exact complexion which the shastras direct, we feel assured that the tranquility of the country would not be disturbed for a single moment. And if the apprehension that the widow, unable to ascend the *burning* pile, might possibly reflect disgrace on the family on the spot destined for immolation, by a change of mind, should in any case induce the relatives to dissuade a female from incurring the risk, the advantage would be entirely on the side of humanity and justice. Considering, as we do, the British Government to be the greatest temporal blessing which Providence has conferred on this country, we cannot give up the hope indeed that, ultimately, Government will abolish entirely a custom which involves the murder of the helpless and the innocent, almost without the shadow of support from the Hindoo superstition itself. The immediate and complete interdiction of force, however, in the act of burning the helpless widow, while it would be in exact unison with that benevolence which distinguishes our sway over these regions, would subject the natives to nothing more than the strict observance of their own rules.*

SECTION III.

Further illustration of the important position that the Suttee, though recommended by some modern Hindoo Writers, is not absolutely enjoined by the most authoritative: and that the usual mode of its perpetration is not sanctioned by Hindoo Writers.

An examination of the shastras on this subject has produced two opposite opinions; the one maintaining that there is no authority for the practice besides that of custom, and the other, that it is positively enjoined by some of their best and most celebrated writers. After perusing the arguments adduced on both sides, we are led to conclude, that the opponents are, in part both right, and both wrong; and that the truth lies in the middle part, and not in the extreme, which each has embraced.

A slight acquaintance with the Hindoo writings may serve to convince any one, that they are capable of being quoted in defence of many things both unnatural and absurd. What Cicero said of the ancient philosophers may, with equal, if not greater truth, be applied to Hindoo authors: "Nihil tam absurdum, quod non dixerit aliquis philosphorum."

It might be expected, on a subject in which life and death are concerned, and which applies to thousands of respectable individuals,

---

the husband is merely an alternative. Hence he argues that the alternative can never have the force of law.

* Friend of India, (mon. ser) Vol. i. page 305—311

that we should have many volumes to read through before we came to a complete knowledge of the matter, and learned all that could be said in its defence; but this is so far from being the case that, to our knowledge, there is not among the multifarious shastras of the Hindoos *a single work written on the burning of widows!* all that is said about it is to be sought for in different authors, and to be found only in broken fragments: it seems that the subject was never regarded in so serious a light as to be thought worthy of being discussed in a separate and distinct treatise. Among a people who have books without number, on the most trifling and impertinent subjects, it appears rather strange that there should be no popular work on this; there cannot surely be needed a stronger proof of the light estimation in which the affair has ever been held by the natives themselves: and from this, we feel convinced, that is has increased to its present inveteracy, more from the force of custom than from any thing that has been advanced in its favour, or been esteemed sacred in the practice.

As the defenders of the practice have abandoned all reasoning on the point, and have betaken themselves to the authority of the shastras as an impregnable fortress, from which they discharge all their artillery, we shall proceed to consider the nature of the materials by which they contrive to destroy widows and create orphans.

It is, alas! too true that passages do exist in the shastras by which this practice is recommended, though not positively enjoined. From the Rigvaid the following passage is quoted, as decidedly in its favour:—

"Let these women, no longer widows, excellent wives, anointed with collyrium and ghee, enter, without tears, without complaints, excellent jewels, let them ascend before the source of beings."

It is supposed that these words are addressed to fire as a god, and that they justify the widow in burning. They do appear to recommend it, though they are certainly far from doing it with that clearness which a case of such importance requires. The words are very dubious, and would admit of other interpretations, just as well as that given by those who quote them in favour of female immolation. It is not unfrequently the case, that words are taken up without due examination, and a certain meaning attached to them which, when examined, is found to be incorrect: we do not say that it is so with the words in question; but, since the meaning of them is doubtful, we infer, that it cannot be a good cause which rests upon them as its chief authority; particularly when there are other passages which afford a refuge from the extreme into which they would lead. The Vishnu Smrite* (or Vishnu Risee, see page 33) shews, that though burning is allowable, it is not necessary:—

"When the husband dies, a retired life, or a funeral pile. Let those who desire it, mortify their body, by living on excellent flowers, roots, and fruits; and let them not pronounce the name of another man after their husband's death."

---

* The Bewasta of the Bengal Pundits presented to Government in 1817, gives this text from this shastra and not from Munoo. (See No. i. Parliamentary Papers printed in 1821, p. 124). Auth.

From these words it is very evident that the immolation of the widow is not peremptorily required by the Hindoo shastras. M*u*noo says, "A faithful wife who wishes to attain in heaven the mansion of her husband must do nothing unkind to him, be he living or dead: let her emaciate her body by living voluntarily on pure flowers, roots, and fruit; but let her not, when her lord is deceased, ever pronounce the name of another man." It is evident that the omission of this cruel ceremony is justified by one of the highest authorities; for the Vaid itself has declared that it is lawful to abide by the advice of M*u*noo.—"Whatever M*u*noo has said that is indeed medicine."

But though M*u*noo is thus celebrated by the Vaid, and his opinion made paramount to that of all others; yet, on this very point, he is contradicted by another writer, who tells us that the case admits of no such remedy as that prescribed by M*u*noo. His words are,—

"There is no virtue known for virtuous women, after the death of their husband, besides that of falling into the fire."

It is difficult to conceive of a more glaring contradiction to the law of M*u*noo; and how are we to reconcile these contradictions? To reconcile them is impossible. What then is to be done? A third writer comes forward to help us over this difficulty, and tells us,—

"The shastra that is opposed to M*u*noo is not to be praised."

By this we understand, that it *ought to be rejected*. From what has been above quoted, it will readily be acknowledged, that the practice is recommended by Hindoo writers, though not in an absolute and peremptory form: it may be omitted, upon the best authority, without any disgrace; and this opens an easy way for setting it aside altogether, because the prohibition of it would not be the repealing of a law, but the enforcing an alternative recommended by the shastras.

We find *no arguments* brought from the shastras to prove the fitness and reasonableness of burning widows, and no effectual attempts made to defend it, against the charge of *self-murder:* this is the more singular, as it seems to be acknowledged that, if the deed be murderous, no advantage will arise from it. This we learn from the following passages:—

"If the husband be out of the country when he dies, and the virtuous one, taking his shoes, purifying herself, enters into the fire, she is not guilty of self-murder according to the Rigvaid." "But the wife of a brahmun must not ascend a separate pile."

We know not whether most to admire, the reasoning or skill of these two passages. The reasoning is, that self-murder does not consist in a woman's killing herself, but in the manner in which she does it; and the skill consists in this, that the wives of brahmuns, by this mode of reasoning, are, in certain cases, saved from a horrid death: though, if it were so honourable a one as they pretend, such honourable characters ought to be among the first to whom it should be appointed. It is argued not to be self-murder for a woman of an inferior caste to burn herself with the shoes of her husband, should he die at a distance; yet this act is forbidden to the wife of a brahmun: and why? Must we conclude, because it would be self-murder in her? The declaring of the one innocent, to whom it is recommended, necessarily supposes the other, to whom it is forbidden, to be guilty, should she perform the same act. Now we ask, what sort of logic is this? Here are two women in exactly the same circumstances, with this only difference, that the one is the wife of a brahmun and the other of a soodra: and if the latter burns herself it is not murder; but if the former burns, we are left from the prohibition to conclude that it is.

It may be replied by the native advocates for the practice, that the difference in their caste is sufficient to explain this inconsistency: but waving all the arguments that might be brought to oppose such a notion from reason and common sense, we maintain, from their own laws, that such distinction does not afford the smallest excuse in their favour; for only suppose the dead husband to be present, instead of his shoes, and then the case becomes quite inverted: then it is not self-murder, but a sublime virtue, for the wife of a brahmun to burn herself; and in so doing she far outstrips in sanctity the wife of the soodra who performs the same deed. How strange, that the presence of a dead body should make such a difference in the nature of a moral action! We may safely defy any one to prove the immutability of truth, if such grounds of argumentation are admitted. How happy a thing would right reason be in this case! Only let it be supposed, that the presence or absence of a dead body can make no difference in the nature of a moral action, and that, if it is wrong for the wife of a brahmun to burn in the absence of her dead husband, it must be wrong also for her to burn in his presence, and this rite would soon cease to exist; for we believe it is through the number of respectable persons of this description who suffer annually that it continues to be held in repute. From the lines which have been quoted, and which are all we know on this part of the subject, we perceive that, so far from vindicating the deed from the charge of self-murder, what has been advanced rather proves such a charge to be correct.

We can find no reason given in the shastras *why the son should set fire to the pile of his own mother:* and were we left to infer from his conduct on the occasion, what his ideas of the act were, we should conclude that he was conscious of his guilt, as he averts his countenance from the horrid sight the moment he applies the flaming torch. This would indicate some degree of feeling, some consciousness of shame and pain; and yet, if these really existed, or at least to any considerable degree, they would surely lead him, not only to avert his head, but at once stand out against the murder of his mother to the very last, though enjoined by all the lawgivers in the universe.*

We think the burning of widows totally inexcusable because it is in direct contradiction to one of the first principles of our nature, self-preservation. God delights in the preservation of his creatures, and that which he delights in must be happy. He has armed all animated beings with a wonderful power, which repels every effort made to destroy life. From the ferocious tiger to the timid hare, we find the same instinctive property of self-defence and love of life. The Divine Being has shewn us, by the instinct which he has implanted in us,

* Asiatic Observer, (April, 1824), No. vi. page 105—110.

by the structure of the various limbs of our bodies, and still more by the reason with which he has endowed us, that it is our indispensable duty to preserve, and not to destroy ourselves; a duty which we cannot violate without incurring his displeasure. So strong is the attachment to life implanted in our nature, that from time immemorial it has been proverbial: "Skin for skin, yea, all that a man hath, will he give for his life:"* and that this powerful principle might act universally and successfully, the God of nature has so formed and disposed of all the members of the human body, as to render them most efficient in defending us against danger; and besides this, he has added to human beings the faculty of reason, to teach them how to use these most efficiently for their own preservation: and thus he has defended, with the strongest barriers, every avenue leading to self-destruction. If we add to these principles of our nature the sanctions of revelation we shall find, that of all the crimes done under the sun, that of self-murder is the most enormous. The Divine law expressly declares: "Thou shalt do *no* murder;" and in this prohibition self-murder must certainly be included. The Gospel, which is a system of mercy, declares it as a thing with which all ought to be acquainted: "Ye know that no murderer hath eternal life abiding in him." Ignorant of these highest of all considerations, and unfaithful to those inscribed on their hearts by the hand of nature, the widows of Hindoos in this country, impelled by false shame, reproach, and the prospect of a miserable existence, break through all the bonds of nature and reason, and throw themselves down to be consumed in the flames with the dead body of their husband. We pity the sufferers, but we must condemn the deed:—

> "Shall Nature, swerving from her earliest dictate,
> Self-preservation, fall by her own act?
> Forbid it, Heaven!"

But there is in this act a violation of the laws of nature, not only on the part of the widow, but also on that of her son, who sets on fire the funeral pile. Nothing can be more evident to a reflecting mind, than that children were designed by Providence to administer to the temporal comfort of their parents. One reason why they are necessitated to be so long dependant on their parents, may be, to impress on their minds a sense of the obligations under which they are laid, to help and console them in return, should they ever stand in need of their succour. All civilized nations have agreed, that it is the duty of a child to honour his parents: hence, when a Grecian lawgiver was asked why he had specified no punishment for the murderer of a parent, replied, that he did not believe such a monster could ever exist; and hence the Romans erected a temple in honour of one who had, in an extraordinary manner, supported a parent, when dying for want in a dungeon. In our own country, if a son, at the time he ought to comfort and sustain his afflicted, sinking mother, should imbrue his hands in her blood, it would be regarded as a crime which no name could designate, and for which no sacrifice could atone. The writer of this very well recollects, that an English child, when he heard the

* This same proverb, though in different words, exists among the Hindoos.

relation of the Bengalees burning their own mothers, very gravely asked: "And, Sir, don't they hang them for it?" We think the natives have no reason to complain of the want of filial affection in their sons, deplorable as it is, while they encourage them to murder their own mothers, at that very important crisis, when they ought to administer to them the balm of consolation. What idea can children possibly have of filial obligations, when, instead of an outrageous crime, it is considered a sublime virtue, for a son to burn his own mother alive?

The unnatural friends who urge the mother and son to the perpetration of the murderous deed, the brahmuns who officiate at the inhuman rite, and the multitude who applaud the act, are all guilty of murder, according to the laws of Munoo; for he states, that in any crime, the instigator, the perpetrator, and the encourager, are equally criminal. If we view things in this light, and consider the number of widows that are annually sacrificed, we shall find that there is no country in all the world so full of murderers and murder as Bengal. It has generally been considered that the burning of a widow is a simple act, which affects only the individual who suffers; but it is not so. How many urge her to it, how many assist her at it, and how many rejoice in it! This swells the enormity of the crime more than a hundred fold, because, instead of the guilt of one or two, it frequently involves the guilt of hundreds, and all these by participating of the crime, are exposing themselves to greater tortures than those of the widow, by "treasuring up to themselves wrath against the day of wrath, and revelation of the righteous judgment of God, who will render to every man according to his work." The deed is still further aggravated by the cruelty which attends it. To strike a female in a civilized country, is reckoned a great disgrace to a man: but what is this, when compared to the cruelty of those, who bind with strong cords the defenceless widow to the dead body of her husband, press her down with still stronger bamboos, lest she should make her escape, put the torch which is to kindle the consuming fire into the hand of her son, and when the smoke and flames ascend to Heaven, drown the shrieks of the dying by loud vociferations, exult as though they had achieved some great exploit, and return home as though they had been to a feast and not a funeral? We can conceive of no murder so aggravated as this. The accounts of cannibals destroying and devouring their enemies, is not half so revolting to the feelings of a man who considers the difference of the two cases. To leave a female unprotected in the hour of danger or distress, is considered a greater act of cruelty than that of destroying a public foe; but because she is unprotected, and because her husband has made no provision for her, to destroy her outright, and that in the most cruel manner, is an act of barbarity to which the annals of time can furnish no parallel. What a striking contrast do we here perceive between the precepts and practice of Hindooism and Christianity! The one teaches us, that "pure religion and undefiled before God and the Father is this, To visit the fatherless and widows in their affliction, and to keep himself unspotted from the world." The other would have us believe, that pure religion and undefiled before God and the Father is this, To burn the widows in their affliction, to render the fatherless still more destitute, and to seek only after the gain of this world.*

From the passage just quoted we learn, that those who assist at these ceremonies, are so far from escaping the charge of murder, that it is irrevocably fixed upon them by their great legislator, who declares, that "*the instigator, the encourager, and the perpetrator, are all alike, either guilty or meretorious.*" Several vain attempts have been made to evade the force of this charge; but it is so plain, so reasonable, and so decisive, that it is impossible for the guilty to escape. If the finding of another passage to contradict this would effect their liberation, they would have some ground of hope; but, when every instance they bring must bow to the decision of Munoo, whose authority is established by the Vaids, their case must be hopeless.

Having ascertained that there is nothing in the shastras which frees the burning of a widow from the charge of murder, and that a way is open for her escape from the devouring flames; we next inquire, whether the circumstances attendant on the rite, are such as are sanctioned by Hindoo writers. It is declared in their writings, that the widow who burned with her husband, in former times, ascended the flaming pile, as may be perceived by these words,—"*She who was devoted to her lord entered the flaming fire.*" It has been thought by some that if the natives were required to attend to the ceremony in this its ancient form, the horrors attending it would be so great, that very few would be found possessed of sufficient resolution to encounter them. If we could estimate the precise point at which a blind superstition would stop, we might determine this matter; but while we remain ignorant of this, we can only indulge in suppositions which experience might contradict. However, if the rite must be attended to, it ought to be performed according to the rules laid down by the authors who recommend it. This, if it did not make fewer sufferers, would probably make a greater number of commisserators; it would kindle a flame of compassion in the hearts of spectators, unless their consciences were seared as with a hot iron, and would lead them earnestly to desire the abolition of so terrible a practice. As the business is now transacted, the most appalling scene is concealed from all but Him, to whose eyes all things are naked and open. And what are the arguments which the natives urge for the violence they use in applying ropes and bamboos to bind and hold down the body, in order to conceal the sufferings of the widows? None at all: they cannot find a single argument in all their books to justify it. Are they then without an excuse? That were impossible. But what can they say, if it is contrary to the shastras? "O it is the custom of their part of the country; it has been done so for many years; it is necessary to secure the prey," &c. After having placed their entire reliance on the shastras for the defence of their conduct, we might leave it to the decision of a child, whether they are justified in the

* Asiatic Observer, (January 1824), No. v. Page 21—24.

adoption of measures which these writings expressly oppose, by prescribing a different line of conduct.

Our next inquiry is, into the motives which the shastras present to the widow to induce her to burn with her husband. The strongest influence which they have over her mind is that which arises from the promises made of future felicity, to be enjoyed by herself and her family in heaven. A few writers are very loud in their praises of this meretorious deed: but when it is remembered, that some are equally loud in their praises of the most insignificant actions, and others totally condemn the motives from which they proceed, such encomiums will appear as sounding brass, and such promises as a tinkling cymbal. The promises made by *U*ngira to the widow who ascends the funeral pile, are thus expressed:—

"The woman who ascends the funeral pile with her dead husband, shall shine as a star with him in Heaven. She who follows her lord shall remain in Heaven as many years as there are hairs on the human body, viz. thirty-five millions. As the snake-catcher draws the serpent from its hole by force, so she, rescuing her husband, rejoices with him. The faithful one who follows her husband, purifies the three families of her mother, father and husband."

Omitting the consideration that these promises are expressed in poetic language, which admits of exaggeration, in order to ascertain how much they should influence the mind, it is necessary for us only to understand the gratuitous manner in which such rewards are offered in the shastras, as we shall then discover, that they may be obtained at *a much less expense than that of life.* If we form our ideas of the merit of a widow's burning from the rewards attached to it, we shall find that it is not so very meritorious as it is generally represented; for nearly the same reward is offered to the person who presents only a single plantain to Seeb.

"He who offers a single ripe plantain to Seeb, shall, with his relations, be exalted to Heaven for thirty millions of years."

The only difference in the reward of the person who offers a plantain, and of her who offers her life, is five million years: the former is to remain in Heaven thirty, and the latter thirty-five million years. If happiness can be thus secured, the sacrifice of life to obtain it can be considered as nothing less than insanity.

But it is to be remembered here, that these promises are made only to those who are not fully acquainted with what they are doing. It seems very reasonable, that the female who has to go through the dreadful ceremony, should have a clear knowledge of what she is about, and a mind well fortified by the authority of the holy books to endure the pain of so miserable a death. No such information, however, is imparted, no such consolation afforded; and what is much worse, they are denied upon the greatest penalty; so that should she aspire after them, and succeed in obtaining them, she would not only destroy the merit of the holy act she was about to perform, but lose the enjoyment of Heaven for thirty-five million years, and sink into Hell. The writings held in the highest repute among the Hindoos are the Vaids; these are said to be to them what the Bible is to

Christians; if so, then as Christians in all their troubles fly to their Bible, so it appears reasonable that these distressed widows should have recourse to the Vaids for consolation. But they are told,

"The woman or the Soodra that understands them, will go to Hell after death."

This shows us how necessary ignorance is to the support of error, and reminds us of those dark days, when the reading of the Bible, by the common people, was thought worthy of present and everlasting destruction.

The idea of the woman's dragging her husband out of Hell, as a snake-catcher draws a serpent out of a hole, is very degrading to the brahmuns. We are constantly taught in the shastras to believe, that the brahmuns are vastly superior to their wives in virtue, and that their attention to religious ceremonies all their lives secures them final blessedness; but now it seems that they sink into Hell after all, and need the assistance of the poor creature whom they have so often spoke of, and treated with contempt, to deliver them out of their miseries: we wonder that the pride of their hearts has not taught them to despise such a means of liberation. We leave it to their sober reflections, whether any thing that has been said of them by others, implicates them in so much disgrace as this verse, which they quote in favour of female immolation.

If the brahmuns, whose widows burn, have not done any thing to secure their salvation during their life-time, they may have died by the side of Gunga, which of itself saves them from going to Hell. What need, therefore, can there be of their wives dying to save them? and how can they be so cruel as to drive the poor helpless widow through flaming fire on earth, and through dismal shades in Hell, in search of one where he is not to be found? May it not be proved, in the clearest manner, from the shastras, that this is *entirely a needless piece of suffering?*

There is yet another consideration, which makes all the promises made to the widow both futile and absurd: which is, that they are not only made without the least evidence of their ever being performed, but are fully contradicted by numberless other passages. On this head the shastras contradict each other in the plainest terms: one says:—

"The widows who follow their husbands in death, are all pure, whether they do it from lust, from anger, from fear, or from folly."

Another says, that "from lust springs sin, and from sin springs death;" and a third informs us, that these rewards are only offered for the allurement of fools:—

"For the sake of alluring those fools who regard only enjoyment, and cannot distinguish between flesh and spirit, (spirit and not spirit,) rewards are offered."

What then does all the suffering of the widow secure to her? It secures her little more than could be attained by offering a single plantain; and she is expressly denominated a fool, if she seeks for happiness by any such means. Is it possible to conceive of more egregious trifling on a solemn subject than this? That a person should be allured by flattering promises to sacrifice her life, to secure a reward either unnecessary, or attainable by the offering up of a single plantain, and then be told that she is a fool for being thus seduced?

Our last inquiry regards what the shastras have said concerning the moral influence of this practice. They have attempted to extol it very highly in reference to the persons immediately concerned, and have asserted, that the merit of the deed is so great, that its influence will extend to the individuals and their ancestors for an almost indefinite period. The very words, however, which they have used to celebrate this conduct, afford to us the plainest proofs of its demoralizing effects. The merit of actions must be estimated by the motives from which they take their rise: hence it is said, that "by God actions are weighed," because he is the only being that can fully comprehend the motives from which they originate. This is a fundamental principle in morality, and a mistake in this must involve serious consequences: to estimate the merit of an action by any other criterion, is like building a house upon the sand. Though this idea is maintained by many of the Hindoo writers, yet in all the calculations that are made respecting the merit of the Suttee, it is entirely left out of the question; and we are told that the deed is still meritorious, though it springs from lust, anger, fear, or folly. Where such a sentiment is maintained, the basis of all morality is necessarily destroyed. What will become of virtue, if by these vices the rewards of virtue may be secured? Can we think of an idea more pregnant with mischief than this; and need we wonder at the conduct of those who adopt it, when they say, "Let us do evil that good may come."

The verse preceding the one which states, that it is of no consequence from what motive the act proceeds, declares that, however unfaithful in heart the woman may have been during her husband's life-time, if she is only faithful at last, all will be well. We ask, what must be the tendency of such a sentiment on the social circle? There is no need, after this, to exhort women to be moral in their conduct: all that is necessary is, to exhort them, should they survive their husbands, to prepare for immediate death, and by one act of faithfulness in their death, to compensate for all the unfaithfulness of their lives. After having freed the woman from all moral obligations during her lifetime, and declared that it is of no consequence from what motives she immolates herself at last, we may indeed wonder what arguments these authors would use to convince them of the necessity of being virtuous.

While the consequences which result from this system to the bereaved families are passed over in silence, those which result to society in general are calculated with no degree of precision. *U*ngira affirms, that this deed will expiate any crime.

"If the man has been the murderer of a brahmun, or ungrateful, or the murderer of his friend, the woman purifies him."

M*u*noo has declared, that the killing of a brahmun is an unpardonable sin, for which their is no expiation. But, passing by these gross contradictions, we would solicit the attention of the reader only to the moral tendency of these words. We should not have supposed that, a people so mild and so averse to murder, as the Hindoos, would have trifled so strangely with the subject, as to suppose that it could be atoned for by the burning of a widow. If one murder can thus expiate another, then we may conclude that any vice will produce its opposite virtue. It is happy for this country, that the general disposition of the natives prevents them from turning such ideas to the mischievous purposes of which they are capable. Had it not been so the community would have been deprived, in numberless instances, of its wisest and most honourable members, and the cords of friendship would have been cut as frequently by death as they are now by quarrelling. We are happy to find ingratitude, in the verse above quoted, ranked among the vices of extraordinary magnitude, and placed by the side of the unpardonable sin, the killing of a brahmun. We had heard it asserted by some, that gratitude was a thing so little known among the natives of Bengal, that they had not a word to express such an idea. This is a mistake; yet what must we think of the extent to which ingratitude prevails, when it is maintained not to be ungrateful for a son to set fire to his own mother? And how are we to account for the extent of this bad principle, but by attributing it to that spurious morality which teaches that any crime may be expiated by the murder of an innocent and helpless widow?

We have now considered all the arguments which the shastras contain on the burning of widows, as far as we are acquainted with them, and as far as the native disputants have been able to draw them from the stores of antiquity. We have not quoted every line they have produced, but we have endeavoured to quote every line that contained a new idea; so that what we have stated may be considered as the substance of what they have to advance on the subject. Had the deed been commanded by the shastras *positively and absolutely*, something might have been pleaded in excuse of the practice; but when a way of escape is opened by one of the highest authorities, the continuation of it, appears to us, an indelible stain upon the Hindoo character, and an unparrelled monument of the effects of superstition.

We have, in the discussion of the subject, exposed only a few of the contradictions of the shastras: were they all pointed out, we scarcely think that writings, which contradict each other on almost every important point in morality, would be acknowledged as the standard of right and wrong in cases where life and death are concerned. That the Hindoo shastras contradict each other on almost every moral subject, is capable of proof, and is acknowledged by a celebrated writer of their own.

"The Vaids are at variance, the Shastras are at variance, and there is no one sage whose system is not opposed by another."

Might we be permitted to suggest an inquiry drawn from this acknowledged fact, it would be this: *When the shastras disagree among themselves, ought not those rules in them to be enforced which are most consistent with moral rectitude, and most conducive to the good of the community.*

We shall conclude this essay by summing up the facts which we are able to substantiate from their own writings relative to the burning of widows.

From the whole we learn these important truths:—That the shastras do not require or command a widow to burn:—that in recommending it they have not taken into consideration whether it is murderous or not, but have expressed themselves so unguardly as to leave the subject fairly open, on their own grounds, to this objection; that in case the woman does not choose to burn, they prescribe methods by which she may obtain future bliss, without the pain of burning:—that should the widow burn, upon the supposition that she is a self-murderer, they involve also, in the charge of murder, the son and the brahmuns that assist her:—that they do not, in the least degree countenance the cruelties which are now practised, in binding the widow to the dead body, and holding her down with bamboos:—that the rewards, though apparently great, and on that account imposing, are little more than are attainable by offering *a single flower or plantain:* —that since, according to the shastras, the brahmuns and their families do not go to hell when they die, there cannot be the least need of the widow's suffering to deliver them:—and that the considerations on which this practice is recommended are such as tend to destroy all morality, and open the door to the commission of the most enormous crimes.*

SECTION IV.

Further discussion of the subject of the two preceding sections; being the Review of a pamphlet on the burning of Hindoo Widows written in Bengalee by a Pundit.

This work, small as it is, is in a high degree interesting, merely from the circumstances in which it appears, and the subject it embraces. It is the product of a native press, and is among the first attempts yet made, for these three thousand years, to appeal to the public respecting the justness and propriety of practices received as sacred by the Hindoos, from their being sanctioned by antiquity. It forms one of the fruits which have arisen from the introduction of printing into India; and is the result of that wise and benign sway exercised by Britain over her possessions in the east. Under the Moosulman or the Hindoo Governments which formerly existed here, nothing of this kind could have appeared: as no one durst venture publicly to question the propriety of any practice which professed to derive its sanction from the Koran, or the Hindoo shastras, its advocates would not have found it necessary to bring any discussion respecting it before the public, much less to submit those arguments on which it might rest for support to public decision.

Such however have been the oblique effects of that diffusion of light which the residence of Europeans has produced in India, that the natives themselves begin to feel the necessity of recurring to reason as the test of their conduct in things both civil and religious. They cannot but perceive that this is the line of conduct observed by

* Asiatic Observer, (April, 1824), No. vi. Page 111—120.

their rulers themselves; that no length of time, no weight of authority, is thought sufficient to support a practice which may be plainly contrary to justice and humanity, and that the inveteracy of any abuse, so far from forming a reason for its continuance, furnishes only stronger motives for its speedy abolition. It was impossible that this should long be altogether without effect on the minds of the natives: they have already begun, in a certain degree, to think for themselves; and the consequence is, that long prescription, in cases decidedly opposed to righteousness, begins in some measure to lose its weight; and while the advocates of humanity lay before their countrymen their reasons for doubting the propriety of usages evidently contrary to its dictates, the supporters of them are constrained, however unwillingly, to meet their opponents in the public area, and submit to the judgment of the spectators the grounds on which they solicit their continued suffrages.

The subject which occupies the attention of the natives in the present instance is one in which humanity is deeply interested. It affects not the colour of a garment or some bodily posture in devotion, but the lives of the most defenceless and the most virtuous class among the natives of India. It involves the fate of all the mothers and daughters in Bengal, who possess any respectability in life;—and the question is, whether superstition shall in Bengal alone consign to the flames, this and every succeeding year, a greater number of innocent victims than were consumed in the fires of Smithfield during the whole reign of bloody Mary, or than disgraced the annals of papal superstition in Britain from its establishment to its downfall;—whether more fatherless orphans shall be deprived in every succeeding year of their only surviving parent and friend, than were thus bereaved in any year of the most tremendous pestilence ever raged in Britain;—or whether the voice of humanity shall triumph over superstition, folly, and cruelty.

The occasion of this pamphlet is as follows: for some time past the burning of such a number of widows annually, has greatly affected the minds of many among the British inhabitants of this Presidency, who have been constrained to witness these melancholy scenes. Previously to the Marquis Wellesley's departure in 1806, Dr. Carey, through the Rev. Dr. Buchanan, submitted to Government three memorials on this subject. The first of these included the practice of exposing infants, which existed chiefly in the north of Bengal; and that of persons devoting themselves voluntarily to death at Saugur Island and in certain other places. The two last practices were abolished by an order of Government; but the burning of widows has been suffered to continue to the present day. In consequence of many Europeans having expressed their surprise and grief at the prevalence of a practice so contrary to humanity, many natives have at length began to reflect on the subject, and to inquire into the grounds on which it is still continued.

In the course of the last year (1818) Ram*a*-mohun*a*-ruy*a* addressed his countrymen on the subject, in a well-written pamphlet, reviewed in our number for December last, in which he insists that the practice has in reality *no foundation in the Hindoo shastras themselves.* To this pamphlet, the work under consideration is an answer drawn up by some of the pundits in Calcutta, who feel unwilling that so laudable a practice as that of burning their widows shall fall into disuse. It is sent forth without a name and without a title page; but from private information, as well as from the pamphlet itself, we find that it is the work of men by no means deficient in learning. It is written in the form of a dialogue between an Advocate for the system of burning widows, under the term "Bidhaok," and an Opponent, here termed "Nishedhok." In the body of the work every authority supposed to countenance the inhuman custom, and every scrap of S*u*ngskr*ita* found on its side among Hindoo writers, are given in the original text, as well as translated into Bengalee. The work is valuable therefore from its containing every thing found in the Hindoo shastras in favour of this barbarous practice; and if all this fall short of an absolute and indispensable injunction, the practice will be found to be as illegal according to the Hindoo shastras, as it is inhuman in itself. This work is evidently intended for the perusal of Europeans also; as an English translation, (if it deserve the name,) is prefixed to the original work. This pamphlet not being put into our hands till the piece on this subject given in our Number for July was put to press, we were unable to notice it at that time. We now however redeem the pledge then given to examine it on the first convenient opportunity; in doing which, while we study brevity as much as possible, we deem it a duty we owe to humanity to attempt it in a manner sufficiently full to enable our readers to judge of the merits of the question, as well relative to the foundation on which it is said to rest in the Hindoo shastras, as respecting the answers here given to the objections urged against the practice by the friends of humanity. In our extracts from this pamphlet we prefer quoting its own language for the sake of doing it every degree of justice, and shall content ourselves with merely adding a sentence or a word where the translation is not sufficiently clear. The work commences by the Advocate's urging the claims of his cause in the following pompous and sweeping declaration.

"It is ordained by (the) Srutee, Smrtee, Pooran*as*, and other sacred books, that the women, on the death of their husbands, should die in Sh*u*h*u*-m*u*r*u*n*a*, that is to burn (should burn) themselves alive with the corpse of their respective husbands; and, that in want of the corpse, (they) should die in *U*noo-m*u*r*u*n*a*, that is to burn, (should burn) with something belonging to their husbands: which usages the great sages during all the four ages of the world, viz. S*u*ttw*a*, Treta, Dwap*u*r*a*, and K*u*lee, have regularly maintained in their codes. It is very improper that you throw obstacles to prevent such a matter." To this the Opponent is made to reply, "You say this is improper for want of knowledge of the shastras or law, but when you know the shastra, you will no more say so."

This forms the signal for the Advocate's unmasking all his batteries and pouring forth on the poor Opponent, every sentence and scrap of S*u*ngskr*ita* in support of the practice, which he had been able to muster up. The chief of these authorities is that of *Ungeera*, who, however does little more than *recommend* the practice. We give his opinion in the Advocate's own translation:—"The woman that mounts the funeral pile of her deceased husband, equals herself to *U*roond-hootee the wife of V*ushisht'ha*, and enjoys bliss in heaven with her own husband. She that accompanies her husband to the other world —dwells in heaven for three and a half cootee years, (thirty-five millions), which is equal to the number of hairs on a human body, and with (by) her own power taking her husband up, in the same manner as a snake-catcher would have taken a snake out of its hole, remains with him in diversion. She that goes with her husband to the other world, purifies three generations, that is, the generations of her mother's side, father's side, and husband's side; and so, she being reckoned the purest and the best in fame among women, becomes too dear to her husband, and continues to divert herself with him for a period equal to the reign of fourteen (successive) Indr*as*; and, although the husband be guilty of slaying a brahmun or friend, or be ungrateful of the past deeds, yet the said woman is capable of purifying him from all these sins. Hence," says the Advocate, "*U*ngeera affirms, that after the demise of a husband, there can be no other duty for a chaste wife than to destroy herself in the fire."

Purasura is then quoted as confirming part of this recommendation, by saying,—"The woman that goes with her husband to the other world, dwells in heaven for three and half cootee years, which is equal to the number of hairs on a human body." *Hareeta* is, after this, introduced as enjoining it by consequence in the following luminous observation: "After the death of a husband, until his wife does not burn (burn) herself in the fire, she cannot get rid of her feminine body." This sentence is to be noticed for the inference which will be found drawn from it in the latter part of the work. The *Muhabharuta* is then adduced as declaring that a woman's burning herself on her husband's funeral pile, atones for her having been a scold or even unfaithful throughout life, and secures her accompanying him in the other world, maugre all unwillingness on his part: and this although she burn herself from "amours, wrath, fear, or affection." The highest countenance given to the practice therefore, by their own writers, (and these appear but four, *U*ngeera, P*urasura*, Hareet*a*, and Vyas*a*,) *amounts only to a recommendation of it* from certain advantages the widow is deluded with the hope of obtaining; that is, the enjoyment of happiness with her husband—by no means to eternity, however, but for as many years as there are hairs on the human body; *after which*, gentle reader, *she must descend to the earth again, and undergo all that vicissitudes of births which, in the opinion of the Hindoos, constitutes future punishment.*

The Advocate for this practice then goes on to notice another authority, that of *Vishnoo-Risee*, who, however, leaves burning *perfectly optional*, in the following language:—"After the demise of a husband, his wife shall either devote herself to Brumh*achurya*, (a life of austerity), or mount the funeral pile of her husband." To do away the force of this option, the Advocate adds, that the choice of a life of austerity would involve in it eight faults or crimes, but which he has not mentioned that the reader might judge of their nature and magnitude; and that even this option is therefore to be rejected; and thus the hapless widow, according to him, must inevitably consign herself to the flames if she would discharge her duty to her deceased husband. He then goes on to state the authority for *Unoo-muruna*, or a woman's burning herself after her husband's death with some article belonging to him! a practice by no means uncommon at the present day. For this he adduces the authority of only a solitary writer the author of the M*u*tsy*a*-Poorana, in these words:—"In case of the demise of a husband in a distant country, the chaste wife should purify her person by bathing, and then, taking her husband's shoes or another thing, enter into a burning pile to be prepared on purpose." This he justifies by saying, that the R*ig*-ved*a* declares such women not to be guilty of self-murder; which plainly indicates, that if this be self-murder, in the opinion of the Hindoos themselves, it would be condemned. Such then is the whole of the countenance this Advocate, on whom it was incumbent to bring forward the strongest authorities for a practice so repugnant to humanity, has been able to adduce from the Hindoo writers themselves; and this, one quotation from *Oosuna*, condemns in the gross,—it is the voice of nature involuntarily speaking:—"*Let not Brahmunees, or wives of brahmuns, suffer death by entering into a separate pile; but for the rest of the women, brahmunees excepted, this law is most preferable.*" Now when it is considered that every authority adduced in favour of this practice is that of brahmuns, for no shoodr*a* has ever yet become authoritative as a man of learning, this decides the matter at once. If it be meretorious thus to ascend the separate funeral pile, why deny this privilege to the daughters of brahmuns? *Why indeed, but because nature spoke in the breast of this writer!* He was a brahmun, and he shuddered at the idea of consigning his daughter to the flames for the sake of a worthless husband, who might perhaps have treated her with neglect and cruelty all his life. The brahmuns of the present day are, however, far more devout; they are unwilling their wives shall be debarred this glorious privilege, and consign them to the flames precisely as they do others: a plain proof, *that a regard for the authority of their own shastras has little to do in continuing this practice;* the motive for this must be sought elsewhere.

But to these quotations from *U*ngeera, Haree*ta*, and P*u*ras*ura*, the advocates for this practice are well aware, are opposed authorities of far greater weight, and such as completely nullify them and forbid this inhuman custom. These it is the grand object of this pamphlet to do away. The Opponent is now made to quote these, therefore, that the Advocate for the burning system may obtain an opportunity of invalidating them. He first adduces the famous legislator *Munoo*, whose authority is paramount to that of every succeeding writer, as prescribing an opposite course for widows in the following language: —"Listen to the law which M*u*noo has prescribed for the husbandless women. 'After the death of husbands their wives should make themselves lean, by living upon sweet flowers, roots, and fruits; never mind the name of a man, and until the time of their respective death with resignation and restriction continue to observe the laws prescribed for Ekp*u*tnees, (those who have married but one husband); that is, they should, with the desire of obtaining the state of chaste women, devote themselves to the law prescribed for Br*u*mhach*u*ry*a*. As thousands of young brahmuns who, before their arriving at full age, devoted themselves to Br*u*mh*a*ch*u*ry*a* and begot no children have gone to S*u*rg*a* or Heaven, the chaste women in like manner, who after their husband's death devote themselves to the law of Brumh*a*ch*u*ry*a*, may attain bliss in heaven, though issueless.' Hence, says the Opponent, M*u*noo has ordained, 'that women, after their husband's death, should spend the remaining part of their lives in Br*u*mh*a*ch*u*ry*a*.' This decision of M*u*noo's the Opponent confirms by adducing the following corroborative declaration from one of the Ved*a*s, 'Know that whatever M*u*noo pronounced, is a medicine for the soul;' and another from *Vrihusputee*, 'A Sreeti inconsistent with that of M*u*noo is not praiseworthy.'

To get rid of this decision of M*u*noo, which *completely forbids the practice*, is the grand object of this work, and for the sake of this alone it is quoted. This the Advocate, knowing that no commentator can erect himself into a law-giver, and abolish the law itself, first attempts by affirming, (that which no one denies), that it is only the Smritee *inconsistent* with M*u*noo which is unworthy of regard; but as a woman can live a life of abstinence and chastity after burning herself, these two of course are not inconsistent! Feeling ashamed of this argument, he quits it, and adducing the following sentence from *Juyminee*, "where there arises an inconsistency among laws, that maintained by many is preferable," attempts to infer, that the *recommendation* of Ungeera, P*u*ras*u*ra, and Hareet*a*, ought to outweigh *the law itself*, enacted by M*u*noo. Deserting this argument as untenable however, he quotes a passage from the R*i*g-ved*a*, recommending the practice of burning, and affirms that the law of M*u*noo on the subject means nothing more than that of a woman who may by any accident be *prevented* from burning herself with her husband, or afterwards with one of his old shoes, ought to devote herself to a life of austerity. The author of this pamphlet, while he professes to set the authority of the R*i*g-ved*a* against that of the great Hindoo legislator, is however well aware that *the Vedas contradict each other on this very point.* That he may in some way or other obviate this discrepancy, so fatal to his argument, he now introduces the Opponent as quoting a well-known passage from the Ved*a* which forbids the burning of widows in the following words:—"As by means of living still, the duties usual and occasional can be performed to purify the mind, and as by hearing of (and) fixing our mind and devoting our soul to Brumh*a* or the Supreme Spirit, we can attain it (final beatitude or absorption in Br*u*mh*a*,) no woman should therefore spend her life, that is, suffer death in hopes of attaining S*u*rg*a* or bliss in heaven." From this the Opponent infers that, as a widow is forbidden to throw away her life with the hope of obtaining connubial bliss for a limited time in heaven, the authority of those who recommend a widow's burning herself with this hope, is completely nullified; and that it is clear by the determination of the Ved*a*, as well as the command of M*u*noo, that a widow ought not to burn herself, but to embrace a life of abstinence and chastity.

This is the doctrine which it is the object of the writer of this pamphlet to overthrow. After the Opponent has thus stated it, therefore, the Advocate for the burning system urges first, that to infer from the authority of M*u*noo and the Ved*a*, that a woman, instead of burning herself, ought to embrace a life of abstinence and chastity, would strip the writings of those who recommend her burning herself of all authority! an overwhelming argument truly. He then adduces a sentence from M*u*noo, to shew that when one Smriti appears to have one meaning, and another a different one, *both are to be held as law!* The plain inference from this would be, that a widow ought to immolate herself on her husband's funeral pile, and to embrace a life of austerity too! To confirm this wonderful exposition, and to preserve the authority of those, who in their zeal for burning, have happened to contradict their own celebrated lawgiver, the Advocate quotes the following contradictory sentence by way of illustration: "In the Ot*i*rat*a*, or the oblations of clarified butter offered to the consecrated fire, the Shorassee* is to be taken; and in the Ot*i*ratr*a* the Shorassee is *not* to be taken." The just meaning of which, contrary Sutras, says he, is, that if in this sacrifice the Shorassee be taken or received, the sacrifice is superlatively meritorious; but if it be not, the deed is still complete and advantageous. From this illustration the writer, in the person of the Advocate, infers, that if a widow wishes to attain connubial bliss in Heaven, she may burn herself; but if she wishes final beatitude, she may embrace a life of abstinence and self-denial; and then adds triumphantly, "See therefore that a woman's burning herself for the sake of connubial bliss in Heaven has no way been forbidden." The whole of this, if it have any meaning, only goes to say, that even by these authorities, if a widow desires final beatitude she is not commanded to burn herself; and that according to them, all *is merely matter of option.* Thus then the whole hitherto advanced by the Advocate for the burning system is, that by their great legislator it is not commanded but forbidden; and by those commentators who abrogate the law they pretend to explain, it is merely *recommended*, and left perfectly optional. But a further examination of the subject will shew, that this recommendation, while viewed by themselves as degrading in the highest degree, is subversive of the whole system of Hindooism. To illustrate this part of the subject, however, it will be necessary to recur for a moment to the creed of the Hindoos relative to future happiness.

The Hindoos throughout India believe the human soul to form an integral part of Br*u*mh*a*, or the Deity, and hence esteem the summit of future bliss to consist in what they deem final beatitude, or absorption into Br*u*mh*a*, of whom they believe their souls to be a part. To the attainment of this, all their endeavours are directed, for the sake of it the most tremendous austerities are performed; and nothing beyond this is supposed to be within the wish of man. But besides this

* Shorassee, the pot containing the clarified butter and other ingredients.

there are, according to their ideas, many heavens or inferior stages of bliss, to be obtained by certain meritorious deeds. None of these, however, is considered lasting; but the duration of every state of bliss is, according to them, proportioned to the merit of the deed of which it is esteemed the reward. After this period is expired, the person is expected to be born on earth again, and to undergo numerous vicissitudes of births till his mind be so purified as to obtain final beatitude or absorption into the deity, which alone secures a person from the misery of future transmigrations. Their state of misery indeed is esteemed no more lasting than that of happiness; but every kind of suffering therein, (for there is supposed to be a great variety,) is supposed to be proportioned in duration to the demerits of the sufferers; after which they also are said to be born again on the earth, and there to undergo all the vicissitudes of transmigration till they become sufficiently pure to obtain absorption into the deity. Hence a woman who may burn herself for the sake of living with her husband in Heaven for a certain period, on its expiration descends to the earth, and, according to the Hindoos, she may be found in Hell in the course of years. For this reason the wise and learned among them treat these evanescent states of bliss with contempt, and contend that nothing is worthy of pursuit but final beatitude or absorption, which puts an end to all future misery. Hence, a woman's burning herself to obtain connubial bliss in Heaven for a certain period, is deemed by them unspeakably inferior to her obtaining final beatitude through a life of abstinence and chastity. The recommendation in which the Advocate triumphs, therefore, even upon his own principles, ought to have been precisely the reverse of what he has made it, since that line of conduct ought to be recommended to all, which is supposed to secure their *highest happiness*.

The Opponent however is represented as approving of this decision; but for the sake of its being answered, he is then made to urge another objection in the following words: "As in various shastras contempt has been poured on actions done from cupidity, a woman's burning herself from such motives is by no means proper." He then quotes the *Kuthopunishut*, as declaring, that while the pursuit of the system of Sacred Wisdom is considered safe, he who pursues the other system which includes a widow's burning herself, degrades his own nature. This he further corroborates by a long quotation from the *Bhaguvut Geeta*, which charges such as follow the system with acting only from cupidity and ambition. This is correct; for these writers who thus recommend the performance of various religious deeds, though done from the basest motives, prescribe certain sacrifices for the sake of obtaining wealth; some to obtain Heavenly bliss, —and some to secure the destruction of an enemy! The whole of this system, therefore, is, by their best writers, regarded as having nothing in it of the nature of virtue; but as being in reality the indulgence of cupidity, ambition, and malice; which dispositions, indicating an impure mind, are the very reverse of that which they deem necessary to final beatitude. Among these the Opponent properly classes a widow's burning herself with her husband's corpse, with the view of enjoying connubial bliss in Heaven for a certain period; and intimates, that if actions of this kind are not evil, they are at least unnecessary. This fires the Advocate for the burning system, who, to overwhelm his adversary at once exclaims, "Listen then to Srutee, (a quotation from the Veda,) 'A man wishing Heaven for himself shall perform Ushwamedha-jauga,' (the sacrifice of a horse;) and again, 'a man wishing Heaven for himself shall perform Jotisuma-jauga' These and other Srutees, are they to lose their *spirits?* that is, to have no effect? Say what is your answer." The Opponent humbly bows beneath the weight of this rebuke, and acknowledges that the Srutee which commend selfish actions are not void and useless, but intended for those who, previously filled with "amours, wrath, and covetousness," are not inclined to enter disinterestedly into the service of the Supreme God; and that without these Srutees enjoining them thus to sacrifice from cupidity or malice, they, freed from all restriction, would be like an elephant without his guide. To prevent this, says he, certain jaugas were ordained to be performed by them; as *sena-jauga*, by one wishing the death of his enemy; *pootrosti-jauga*, by one longing for a son; and *jotistuma-jauca*, by one wishing bliss in Heaven. This appeases the Advocate, who having thus secured the validity of these commands for performing devotional acts from cupidity, ambition, or malice, admits, that while these deeds are good, still actions done from superior motives are somewhat more praise-worthy. This concession, which might seem unguarded, is in reality made with the view of enabling the Opponent to bring out the last objection he has left, that the Advocate may demolish it like a man of straw. This is couched in the following words:—

"*Nessedhok.* If you maintain that the disinterested actions are better than those self-interested, why do you then, instead of permitting husbandless women to adopt the law of (disinterested) Brumhachura, which gives final beatitude, endeavour to preserve the system of self-interested actions of Shuhu-muruna and Onoo-muruna, which produce (merely) bliss in Heaven?"

This argument, which the Advocate was aware must appear on the face of the subject, and must weigh in favour of a life of abstinence and chastity in preference to burning, as much as eternal beatitude is to be preferred to a continual vicissitude of misery, he now proceeds to obviate. This he first attempts by urging that a woman in embracing a life of abstinence and chastity would still do it with a view to final beatitude, and therefore from self-interested motives: hence as burning herself would also rescue her husband from the pit he might be driven into for slaying a brahmun, or a friend, or being ungrateful, together with the three generations before-mentioned, and enable the woman to "get herself rid of her feminine sex," he esteems it far more desirable that she should burn.

To this conclusive argument the Opponent replies, "Now your sayings are consonant with the shastras." Still, however, he suggests the *probability* of women's attaining the state of final beatitude, were they, after the death of their husbands, "to be disciplined in sacred wisdom, which, by burning themselves, they can never attain." To this the

Advocate for the burning system has an unanswerable argument ready, that all instruction would be totally vain; for, says he, it would be attended with no other success than to condemn them for both the one and the other," in other words, either they would not live the life of chastity recommended, or they would be too dull to do it from proper motives. He concludes the argument with saying, "It is therefore very improper that the women who have never been conscious of so much as the meaning of the word wisdom, shall (should) be desired to follow the system of sacred knowledge." No other mode remains for the poor creature, therefore, but that of preventing their going astray,—or of living chastely from wrong motives, by previously burning them alive. The Opponent is now completely silenced, and at once gives up his argument.

We have now before us the actual grounds on which all those who oppose the abolishment of the practice, still desire to preserve this privilege of *burning alive their mothers, their sisters, and their daughters.* It is not because it is sanctioned by the Hindoo law, for their greatest legislator, whose authority is paramount to every other, *positively forbids it* by enjoining on widows a contrary course. It is not that those few writers who have recommended the practice (for none of them have had the audacity to *command* it in opposition to their great legislator,) recommend it as a superior course, the dictate of more exalted virtue, for they themselves despise the course they thus recommend to the poor widow, and regard with the utmost contempt the motive and principle of action they endeavour to infuse into her mind. But this *unparralleled course of murder* is practised *wholly* as a PREVENTATIVE! But as a preventative of what? the effects of their dulness! their inability to comprehend "the instructions of Sacred Wisdom!" What then would be these effects? That they would live a life of abstinence and chastity from improper motives, from a desire after final beatitude! and thus losing final beatitude, only obtain heaven. Truly their thus forcing their burning system on the poor widow, from principles of such exalted benevolence, outdoes all that the Roman Catholics have ever done in the way of burning heretics out of pure pity to their souls. Yet what does this burning system itself profess to hold out to the poor widow; Only a little evanescent bliss for a limited time. As for the other part, the poor widow's dragging her murderous or ungrateful husband out of the hands of *Yuma*, as a snake-catcher drags a snake out of his hole, it were much better not done. If he has died under the dominion of such barbarous, or base and ungrateful dispositions, it were better far to leave him in the hands of *Yuma* for a season, to be taught better principles, than to take him with her to heaven with these feelings of ingratitude, barbarity, and murder, remaining within him. A wretched heaven indeed she would be likely to experience with such a monster during these thirty-five millions of years. If he did not *murder* her there, it would be merely because she could not become mortal again, till she had worn out this long period of misery. What then is even pretended as the superior advantage of burning? Nothing: while on their own principles it is optional, the option is quite against the widow's interests. By chusing a life of abstinence and chastity, she may attain final beatitude, and even, according to them, she secures a certain degree of bliss, though she should be so dull as to forfeit final beatitude through living with this alone in view; while they allow that final beatitude can never be obtained by her burning herself. But is it to be endured that a poor widow should be burnt merely on account of dulness and stupidity? Is it thus that their mothers and sisters are to be treated? Would they not shrink at burning alive even a beast on the funeral pile of its master? Surely it is horrid beyond expression that relatives so dear should be urged to the burning pile to prevent their living a chaste and virtuous life from a wrong motive merely through dulness, and at the same time be told that it is improper to offer them the least instruction on a subject so important, because they do not as yet know the meaning of the word wisdom.

But this honest declaration that their chief motive for supporting this system of burning is furnished by women's dulness and stupidity, brings to light a part of the creed of these advocates for matricide, which few ever suspected to belong to Hindooism. The whole of the sex, every mother, and sister, and daughter, are hereby doomed to *interminable misery*, since they are declared to be such that it would be improper for them even *to be desired* to follow that system of sacred knowledge universally esteemed by the Hindoo writers *the only path* to final beatitude. Astonishing! We have heard that Moosu*l*mans exclude women from the felicity of the blessed, but this is entirely under the idea of their being without a soul. But if Hindoo women have no souls, what part of them is to enjoy this Heaven of bliss with their husbands for thirty-five millions of years? If, in the delicate language of Hareet*a*, already quoted, "until the wife does not burn (burn) herself in the fire, she cannot get rid of her feminine body," then by that act she does get rid of her body; else, what avails this murderous rite? But if she then gets rid of her body, what is left of her? a soul, a spirit; of course nothing else. But of what materials is this soul or spirit formed? Do they suppose it to be formed of matter, or to be a part of the Eternal Spirit? If they say it is formed of matter they degrade their daughters, and sisters, and mothers, beneath the very beasts around them; for there is not a dog that passes by, a reptile that crawls on the earth, or a jackal that howls by night around their cottage, which they do not suppose to be animated by a portion of the Eternal Br*u*mh*a*. But if they allow that they have souls, and still cannot obtain final beatitude by burning themselves, then this system, while it devotes their bodies to the most cruel death, *dooms their souls to interminable misery*. To what absurdity —to what contradiction even of the whole system of Hindooism, have these advocates for burning their mothers and sisters reduced themselves! After all their pleadings for tenderness to their religious prejudices, it appears evident that this murderous practice is not more contrary to humanity than it is subversive to their own religious dogmas.

But perhaps these advocates for the burning system will urge, that the fear of the poor widow's mistaking through dulness the way to final beatitude, and only reaching heaven, is not the only reason which makes them so desirous of sending her through the flames to enjoy connubial bliss with her deceased husband, that is rather the fear of something worse. This indeed is strongly hinted by the Advocate, in his reply to the Opponent on his expressing his hope that were widows after their husband's death disciplined in sacred wisdom, they might attain final beatitude, which by burning themselves with their husbands they can never attain. In this reply he, declaring that the attempt would be vain, adds "as you say (advise us,) to discipline them in the sacred wisdom, it would be attended with no other success than *to condemn them for both the one and the other.*" But in what way could their being permitted to live and receive instruction condemn them for both the one and the other; or, in other words, cause them to lose every hope of bliss? Their dulness, even in living a life of abstinence and chastity from an improper motive, could only make them fall short of final beatitude; what then should condemn them to the loss of all felicity? The meaning is self-evident: the writer intends to say, that instead of persevering in a life of chastity they might possibly go astray and thus incur the condemnation hinted, which, indeed, nothing but a deviation of this nature could make them incur, since he has already declared, that deeds done from the meanest motive, from "amours (or concupiscence), anger or fear," are still available in the case of a woman's burning herself; and hence the merit of a life of self-denial and chastity cannot of course be destroyed by its motives. He evidently means to say, that as they *would not* live a life of chastity, their burning themselves is the only *preventive* of their utter condemnation. And have they then this shocking idea of their own daughters, and sisters, and mothers? Will nothing preserve them in widowhood from a life of lewdness but their being burnt alive? Then a Suttee at once loses both its name and its nature. It is no longer the effect of chaste affection; it is *the highest dishonour to every family in which it may happen.* It proclaims in the loudest manner that, in the opinion of her own relatives, the sister or the mother who is the victim, *is so corrupt in her disposition, so impure in her mind, that they have no method of keeping her from a life of unchastity but that of burning her alive;* for what person, who had not the heart of a tiger, would resort to this dreadful remedy with so near a relative, while any other course held out the least hope?

But granting all this, still is it right that *this preventive measure* should be adopted with any one, much less with such near relatives? Is it agreeable to natural equity that a person should be burnt alive, not *for* impurity of conduct, but *to prevent it?* If it be, ought it to be confined to one sex? ought it not to be extended to the other likewise, or are the mothers and sisters of those who uphold the burning system more depraved than all who dwell around them? Surely, if this *preventive course* be allowable at all, it ought not to be confined to the most virtuous, merely because they are the most defenceless; it ought to be extended farther, to the *advocates* of the measure themselves. If they do not discover an equal disposition to impurity with their mothers and sisters, they may to other vices equally injurious to society, and according to their own creed equally punishable in the other world. The same *preventive* therefore might with equal benevolence be exercised on them at stated periods, or at least on such of them as seem most likely to perpetrate vice; and if they were less fond of the burning system than they say the poor widow is, they might be permitted to chuse any other mode of dying, and thus the city and the country would, in due time, be purified in the most effectual manner; it might, 'tis true, be somewhat thinned of inhabitants; but the purity of those left behind, and the reflection that all either burnt or hanged on this *preventive system*, were as assuredly in the enjoyment of bliss they would have forfeited by living, as the immolated widow is in the enjoyment of bliss in heaven with her deceased husband, might well reconcile us to the fewness of our neighbours.

The author of this pamphlet having thus far silenced the Opponent, now attempts to justify their binding the poor widow fast to the corpse of her deceased husband, their heaping wood upon her and pressing her down with bamboos. For this purpose he makes the Opponent, after acknowledging that the Advocate for the system had given "the just sense of various shastras," observe, that instead of causing the women to mount the burning pile as the laws direct, they make them first mount the pile, and then, "having strongly tied the said widows to the corpse of their husbands, heap them over and over with wood and large bamboos, and setting fire thereon, burn them to death. We proclaim," adds he, "that you must not slay women in such a manner" To this the Advocate for the burning system does not reply by denying the truth of this shocking fact, or by urging that it is too strongly stated; but he defends it by saying that "in whatever country the practice is to mount the full burning pile, there it is indisputable, (indisputably right); but that in those countries where this is not the practice, this following of local custom is not inconsistent with the shastras, quoting several authors to shew, that the usages and customs of a country ought to be observed. The Opponent is then made to reply that, by this rule, those who, residing in forests and mountains make it their profession to kill living creatures, are to be held blameless. "By no means," says the Advocate, "for the actions of these rude foresters are not approved by men of fidelity, and the laws on the head of Sh*uhumuruna* have been regularly maintained by the holy sages, philosophers, and the learned." The plain meaning of this is, that the learned have themselves introduced into Bengal this custom of firmly binding women to the corpse of the deceased husband, heaping wood on them, and pressing them down with large bamboos from a regard to the custom of the country, when no such custom existed till created by them! In Bengal there was formerly no custom of this nature existing; and had there been, the customs of the rude and ignorant are here said to be unworthy of regard; it is the learned alone therefore who have introduced this inhuman deviation from their own shastras, for which they now plead because it does exist!

The manner in which the Advocate justifies their violating the woman's promise to *mount the burning pile*, however, is still more singular. It must here be remarked, that the woman, before she burns, pronounces what is termed the S*u*nk*u*lpa, which is couched in the following terms:—"*I will mount the* BURNING *pile.*" Adverting to this the Opponent says, "How can the S*u*nk*u*lp*a* be completed, because (when) it is pronounced with a promise to *mount* a burning pile? instead of which they mount it before it touches fire." This difficulty the Advocate removes in a moment. Says he, "Whatever you say regarding the incompletion of the S*u*nk*u*lp*a* arises from your inattention; for should a little part of a village or a cloth be consumed by fire, it is then said, even by learned men, that the village or cloth was (is) burnt. In the same manner a little burning-pile is also called a burning pile, and in that case the S*u*nk*u*lp*a* was (is) not incomplete." As much as to say, that if a single twig be set on fire, this constitutes a burning pile! In this manner do these men, with the most daring effrontery, *sport with their violating even their own most sacred formulas, for the sake of securing the destruction of a poor defenceless widow, in whom nature might otherwise recoil at the doom awaiting her.*

The next reply, however, is, for its *levity* and *falsehood*, if possible, *still more disgusting.* The Opponent is made to answer, "I approve of your saying this; but from what instances the people attending funeral ceremonies (by what authority do the people attending funeral ceremonies) tie up the women that are about to mount the burning pile? and why are they not guilty of the sin of slaying women?" To this the Advocate replies, "In the aforesaid text of *Hareeta* it was (is) expressed, that until the women themselves cause their bodies to be consumed in the fire, they cannot finally get rid of their sex. In which case, should any part of their bodies, while burning asunder in the piles (on the pile) *be slipped out thereof, it cannot be wholly consumed.*" It is difficult to say whether the *indelicacy*, the *shocking levity*, or the *impudent falsehood* of this reply be most to be detested. Granting that the *horrid rite* requires every particle of the body of the wretched victim to be consumed, does their binding her secure this? It secures her *death* it is true; it renders all the recoilings of nature unavailing; but do they bind down every limb of their helpless victim? if they did, would not the cords be the first fuel for the flame? For men *thus to sport with decency, humanity, and truth, in defence of* MURDER *offered to a British public, is of itself sufficient to condemn for ever the* INHUMAN CUSTOM. We shall only detain the reader with one instance more of this kind. The Opponent having expressed his approbation of this reason for binding women, has only one scruple left, which is, whether those who assist in burning the widow are not guilty of sin. To this the Advocate for burning replies, that it rather exalts them to glory than renders them guilty of sin, which he confirms by reciting the following example from *Mutsya-poorana*, "There was a prostitute named Leelav*u*tee, who having resolved to make an offering of an artificial salt-hill, one goldsmith, named Heemt*u*r*u*gh*u*tuk*a*, undertook the work, and perceiving it to be a divine action he took nothing from the girl for his hire, but constructed for her a salt-hill with so much elegance and neatness that afterwards, in reward thereof, the said poor and theological goldsmith together with his wife was endowed with immense riches, and became himself the monarch of the seven-dweep*a* universe, with a shining form equal to the rays of ten thousand suns." Hence he gives the Opponent to understand, that whoever assists in burning a widow is likely to reap glory, as well as this theological goldsmith for assisting the prostitute in her devout offering. Thus do the supporters of this system, by the *most idle fables*, as well as the *most indecent examples*, trifle with the *real murder* of their nearest female relatives.

On this subject, as the only reason why this murderous custom is still permitted to pollute the land with blood, when the exposure of infants, and men's voluntarily devoting themselves to death, have been abolished by public authority, must be sought in the idea entertained that it is indispensibly enjoined by the Hindoo laws and system, we intreat permission to subjoin a few extracts from a document in our possession, drawn up in S*u*ngskrit*a* about two years ago by M*ri*tyoon-j*uya*-Vidyal*u*nk*ura*, the chief pundit successively in the College of Fort William, and in the Supreme Court, at the request of the Chief Judge in the Sudder Dewanee Adawlut, who wished him to ascertain, from a comparison of all the works extant on the subject, the precise point of law relative to burning widows, according to those who recommend the practice. This document, as the Compiler of it, from his own extensive learning and the assistance of his friends, had an opportunity of consulting more works on the subject than almost any pundit in this Presidency, may be regarded as possessing the highest legal authority according to the Hindoos. After having consulted nearly thirty works on the subject, current in Bengal and the northern, western, and southern parts of Hindoostan, among which are all those quoted for the practice by the author of this pamphlet, he says, "Having examined all these works and weighed their meaning, I thus reply to the questions I have been desired to answer.—The Juttee Mulla Bilas shastra directs the following formula to be addressed to the bride by the priest at the time of marriage, 'be thou perpetually the companion of thy husband, in life and in death.' Hareet*a*, a later writer, says that it is the inheritance of every woman belonging to the four casts, not being pregnant or not having a little child, to burn herself with her husband." The Compiler afterwards quotes *Vishnoo-moonee* as speaking thus, "'let the wife either embrace a life of abstinence and chastity, or mount the burning pile;' but he forbids the latter to the unchaste." He then enumerates particularly the various rules laid down by him and others who have followed him on the same side of the question, relative to the time and circumstances in which a woman is permitted to burn herself, and in what cases she is even by them absolutely forbidden. These extracts shew that binding the woman, and the other acts of additional cruelty which the author of this pamphlet justifies, are totally forbidden. The *Soodheekoumoodee* as quoted by the Compiler says, "Let the mother enter the fire after the son has kindled it around his father's corpse; but to the father's corpse and the mother let him not set fire: if the son set fire to the *living* mother he has on him the guilt of murdering both a woman and a mother." Thus the possibility of a woman's being bound to her husband's corpse is taken away: while the act is left perfectly optional, *the son is not to be, in the least degree, accessary to the mother's death;* if she burn herself at all, it must be by throwing herself into the flames already kindled. And the *Nirnuya-sindhoo* forbids the use of any bandage, bamboos, or wood, by way of confining the woman on the funeral pile; nor before she enters it must the least persuasion be used, nor must she be placed on the fire by others. Thus the practice as existing in Bengal and defended in this work *is deliberate murder*, even according to the legal authorities which recommend burning as optional.

Mrityoonjuya however shews, from various authors, that though burning is termed optional, it is still not to be recommended. To this effect he quotes the *Vijuyuntee*, "While Brumh*a*chury*a* and burning are perfectly optional, burning may arise from concupiscence, but Br*u*mh*a*chury*a* cannot; hence they are not equally worthy, how then can they be equally optional? By Brumh*a*chury*a* the widow obtains bliss though she have no son." He then quotes several authors, as declaring, that women ought not to burn, because it is merely a work of concupiscence; the *Julwa-mala-vilas* and others as declaring that the practice is merely the effect of cupidity, and not the fruit of a virtuous and constant mind; and the *Mitakshura* as declaring, that by embracing a life of abstinence the widow, by means of divine wisdom, may obtain beatitude; and hence, that a woman's burning herself is improper; adding, that in former ages nothing was heard of women's burning themselves: it is found only in this corrupt age.

The following is the conclusion drawn by this able pundit and jurist from the perusal of the whole of these works. "After perusing many works on this subject, the following are my deliberate and digested ideas: V*i*shnoo-moonee and various others say, that the husband being dead, the wife may either embrace a life of abstinence and chastity, or mount the burning pile; but *on viewing the whole I esteem a life of abstinence and chastity, to accord best with the law;* the preference appears evidently to be on that side. Vyas*a*, Sungkoo, *U*ngeera, and Hareet*a*, speaking of widow's burning, say, that by burning herself with her husband she may obtain connubial bliss in Heaven; while, by a life of abstinence and chastity, she, attaining sacred wisdom, may certainly obtain final beatitude. Hence to destroy herself for the sake of a little evanescent bliss, cannot be her duty; burning is for none but for those who, despising final beatitude, desire nothing beyond a little short-lived pleasure. Hence I regard a woman's burning herself as an *unworthy act*, and a life of abstinence and chastity as highly excellent. *In the shastras appear many prohibitions of a woman's dying with her husband, but against a life of abstinence and chastity there is no prohibition.* Against her burning herself the following authorities are found. In the Meemangshad*u*rsh*u*n*a* it is declared, that every kind of self-inflicted injury is sin. The Sankhy*a* says, that a useless death is undoubtedly sinful. The killing for sacrifice commanded by the shastras has a reasonable cause, and is yet sinful in a certain degree, because it destroys life. And while, by the Meemangsha, either of the two may be chosen; by the Sankhya, a life of abstinence and chastity is alone esteemed lawful. But by the Vedanta, all works springing from concupiscence are to be abhorred and forsaken; hence a woman's burning herself from the desire of connubial bliss, ought certainly to be rejected with abhorrence."

He further adds, "No blame whatever is attached to those who prevent a woman's burning. In the shastras it is said, the Kundurpa being consumed to ashes by the eye of Shiva, his wife, Rutee, determined to burn herself; and commanded her husband's friend, Mudhoo, to prepare the funeral pile. Upon this the gods forbad her; on which account she desisted, but by Kalee-dasa no blame is attached to them for this conduct. Thus also in the *Shree-Bhaguvuta:* a woman, Kripee, had a son, a mighty hero, from love to whom she forbore to burn herself with her husband; yet she was deemed guilty of no sin therein. Now also we hear of sons and other relatives attempting to dissuade a woman from burning; yet they are esteemed guilty of no crime. It is also evident that a woman, in thus burning herself, dies merely from her own self-will, and from no regard to any shastra; such the command of a thousand shastras would not induce to die. They merely reason thus, 'By the death of my husband I have sustained an irreparable loss; it is better for me to die than to live;' hence a woman determines to die: and her relatives seeing this mind in her, provide the funeral pile, and say, "if you are determined to die, to die by falling from a precipice would be tedious, die in this manner:" thus a father who has a son determined to go to a distant country, finding all dissuasion vain, at length sends a guide with him who knows all the rivers and dangerous places. The various shastras therefore describe this action as being merely that of one who, having received an incurable wound, is determined to die, whether by falling from a precipice, by fire, or by water."

After this full and accurate investigation by one so able and possessing such opportunities, the subject, as far as relates to the law of the Hindoos, or to the countenance it receives from the Hindoo system, may well be supposed to be fully before the public. All that the author of this pamphlet, assisted by all the pundits who wish for the continuance of the practice, has been able to bring forth as at all countenancing it, is confined to the opinions of five or six authors, amidst that multitude included by the Hindoos under the term of "the learned:" and after the examination of nearly thirty works written either for or against this practice, the hope of obtaining further light respecting it from the Hindoo shastras, is totally vain. A work to be ranked as an authority in point of law, must have been known and read for ages: any work therefore on the subject hitherto hidden, and hereafter brought forth to countenance the practice, becomes, for that very reason, of no authority. The question is now left to be determined wholly on the principle of equity and reason. It is possible that this practice might have originated in the injunction of the shastra addressed by the priest to the bride in marriage, "Be thou the companion of thy husband in life and in death." It is evident that Munoo was ignorant of the custom of Suttee, by his prescribing for widows a life of abstinence and chastity. From this, however, certain succeeding writers, Hareeta, and some others, may have taken occasion to recommend the widow's burning herself, with the hope of living again with her husband for a limited number of years. But even by these it was enjoined, that this should be a perfectly voluntary act, voluntary in its origin, and in every stage of it; and that this should be manifested by her ascending the *burning* pile without the least force, and by no force being used to detain her there. And should nature recoil at the sight of the flames, the atonement was only three kahuns of cowries, or about *twelve annas*; after which it is expressly enjoined, that she shall be received and treated by her neighbours precisely as before. Above all, the son is forbidden, in the most express manner, to be in the least degree accessary to his mother's death. If frantic grief urge her to put an end to her own existence, it must be by her throwing herself on the funeral pile of her deceased lord, in which she must be no more assisted than as though she were precipitating herself from a precipice. While nothing can be more murderous, therefore, than the practice and mode justified by the writer of the pamphlet under consideration, nothing can be more contrary to the spirit and intention of even those few Hindoo writers who have recommended the burning system.

While this horrid practice is allowed to have been recommended by certain writers, it is evident that it was never considered as a *law*, or as a religious injunction essential to the duty of a good Hindoo. If it be a law binding even in point of conscience, the greater part of India must ever have lived in a state of direct disobedience to the laws of their own religion; for as the recommendation is directed to widows of every cast down even to the lowest, that of a Chandala, it must have been imperative on all, at least as matter of conscience. Yet, not to advert to what Mrityoonjuya has advanced, that it was unknown in the first and purest ages of Hindooism, if the number of widows burnt in Bengal annually do not exceed a thousand, it must be disobeyed even in Bengal, where it is most prevalent, by at least ninety-nine out of a hundred of the population, and in the western part of Hindoostan by a still greater proportion; while, in the southern part of the British dominions, it is said to be scarcely regarded at all. If this practice therefore form a part of the Hindoo religious system, with the exception of one in perhaps a thousand, this system is, by themselves, universally discarded and treated with contempt.*

This barbarous practice, however, while recommended by a few among the Hindoo writers, has been found by others to involve principles directly subversive of Hindooism itself. Here it is almost need-

* "Supposing the entire Hindoo population of the Bengal Presidency to be 50,000,000, and the annual deaths to be 1 in 33, or above 1,500,000 a sixth of this number, or 250,000 might, on a general computation, be assumed as the number of Hindoo females becoming widows, of whom little more than 600 devote themselves on the death of their husbands."
—(*Parliamentary Papers*, *July*, 1825, p. 11.)—Ed.

less to inform the reader that the learned among the Hindoos have been, for numerous ages, almost as much divided respecting their religious sentiments as were formerly the learned of Greece and Rome. One grand principle of the Hindoo system is, that life must not be destroyed: hence their abstaining from animal food; and hence many have thought it sinful to destroy a noxious or a poisonous reptile. Even sacrifices are supposed to involve a certain degree of guilt, as far as they destroy life, although their being done in obedience to a supposed command, causes the merit of the deed to overbalance its demerit. But it is evident, from what has been already urged, that a woman's burning herself has never been considered as a deed *commanded.* Hence, as Mr*i*ty*oo*nj*u*y*a* justly observes, no blame has ever been attached, by any of their writers, to those who have prevented its being done; which would have been the case had it been regarded as a religious duty. Instances enough may be found in the Hindoo shastras of the strong sense they have of the sin of obstructing or preventing a religious act; many examples are related of men said to be destroyed by devotees for interrupting them only in their evening ceremonies. While, therefore, it has been merely recommended by a few, others have beheld it as destroying life without cause, and thus violating one of the fundamental principles of Hindooism.

But many have gone farther, and condemned the *very principle* on which it has been recommended. The ground of this has been already mentioned. The Hindoos maintain, in all its strictness, the doctrine of the metempsychosis, and believe that the human soul is part of the Supreme Being, and that while its desires are impure and corrupt, it can never be re-united to him and obtain final beatitude. Others among them, however, hold that certain deeds, though done from the most unworthy motives, are in themselves so available as to merit a certain degree of recompense; never final beatitude indeed, but wealth, a son, long life, the destruction of enemies, or a certain temporary state of bliss in their Sw*u*rg*a*, or heavens. In this class those rank who contend for the burning of widows, as is sufficiently testified by one of the quotations given in the pamphlet under consideration, which says, that though a woman burn herself from "amours, anger, fear, or affection," she is still certain of obtaining heaven. But all these deeds the more learned treat with the greatest contempt, declaring them to be nothing more than vice in another shape, the indulgence of a corrupt mind. These writers therefore view a woman's burning herself as perfectly unlawful. Thus those who form the great support of the Hindoo system, totally condemn the very principle on which the practice is at all recommended, and esteem the whole an indulgence of vicious and corrupt desires, while they insist, on the other hand, that the law *commands* a widow to live a life of abstinence and chastity. That these compose the greater part of the Hindoos, may be inferred from the proportion of widows thus burnt alive when compared with the whole population of Hindoostan, the horrid practice prevailing chiefly in the lower part of Bengal, and most of all, within about twenty or thirty miles of Calcutta.

Such then is the real state of things relative to this practice, even when described by its most strenuous advocates; for the reader will have seen that in the pamphlet under consideration, the admissions of the Advocate for its continuance condemn the practice scarcely less than Mrityoonjuyu himself. As a *command* it has not the least foundation in the Hindoo system; for while it is *recommended* to all, at least ninety-nine out of a hundred of the strictest and most devout Hindoos have ever lived in complete disregard of it. Had it been otherwise indeed, as the recommendation is general, the country must have been every year a scene of general massacre. If the number of Hindoos in India be computed at a hundred millions, and few will estimate them lower, the least number who die annually must, in the common course of mortality, be estimated at *three millions;* and, as nearly every man is married, and in general to a woman far younger than himself, *a million of widows annually* is the very lowest number which we ought to reckon. Now if only one out of a hundred of these are burned, this will exhibit *ten thousand widows consigned to the flames every year!* but, were the whole million to be thus burnt alive, this country would yearly present such a Gehenna —such a sacrifice to Moloch, as the world has never beheld. A law, however, regularly disobeyed by ninety-nine out of a hundred of those to whom it is given, and this without either punishment or blame, is totally unworthy the name. Such is not the case with the *laws* of the Hindoo system: by these widows are forbidden to marry again,—and not one in a thousand ever marries again. As a *recommendation* then it has not been supported by one fifth of the Hindoo writers on ethics or jurisprudence, nor practically regarded by a thousandth part of those who profess Hindooism. The recommendation is also in *direct opposition* to the command of the great Hindoo lawgiver, who enjoins on every widow a life of abstinence and chastity; and further, it is grounded on principles completely subversive of the Hindoo system, and opposed to that course which the Hindoos believe to be the only path to final happiness. Yet this practice, thus opposed to their great legislator's command—to the very nature of their religious system— and to all their best ideas of virtue, is kept alive in the metropolis and its vicinity by acts of unfeeling coercion, which are the most direct violations of the rules laid down by those few who have at all recommended the practice, while in the provinces of Hindoostan, which is held to have been the chief seat of every important transaction detailed in their mythology, and which contains a brave, noble, courageous race, before whom the natives of Bengal have always trembled, the practice, if formerly prevalent in any great degree, has at this time nearly expired beneath the feelings of common humanity. Yet all these circumstances of additional cruelty are now detailed and justified in an address to the British public, while not the least shadow of argument is brought forward in support of the system; but rather principles are tacitly avowed as the grand motive for continuing it, which discover the most complete absence of feeling for the moral welfare of their dearest female relatives, and reflect on their characters the highest dishonour.

While the discussion of the subject was confined to the native language, a certain degree of silence might perhaps have been less blameable. But after a justification of the system has appeared in the shape of an appeal to the public both in India and in Britain, in the English language, it would be crimiual to remain silent, and a grievous offence against humanity to treat the subject in a light and cursory manner. And when it is considered, that this practice causes the death of a greater number of persons in one year, who, *if they ought not to be thus burnt alive*, involve the country in all the guilt of innocent blood, than are publicly executed for their crimes throughout the whole of India in the course of twenty years, it cannot be wrong to call to this momentous subject the attention of every friend to his country. How would Britain feel, if within herself a hundred innocent persons suffered death by some mistake of law in the course of a year! How then ought she to feel when in only one province of her foreign dominions nearly a thousand innocent widows are every year burnt to death? Were this inhuman persecution, which, in the number of its annual victims, exceeds all that papal superstition ever brought to the stake in Britain in the course of a century, directed by the supporters of this practice against any particular *sect*, or class of men, they would long ago have appealed to their rulers for redress, or they would have left the spot where they were treated with such cruelty. But how can mothers and sisters make an appeal against their own relatives? How can a wife, a mother, withdraw from her own family? They may endure continual agony under the apprehension of the dreadful doom which they know awaits them on the first fatal attack of disease on their husbands,—they may feel their anguish renewed at the sight of every female neighbour they behold led forth to the flames—they may tremble at every touch of disease that affects their husbands, and weep at every recollection of their hapless children;—but can they leave the scene of suffering? can they make *known* their sorrows? dare they bewray, even in the slightest degree, the anguish which preys on their vitals? They lie bound as sheep for the slaughter;—and thus they must remain, suffering in silence, till *British feeling and sympathy shall duly realize* their hitherto unknown, unpitied misery.*———————

SECTION V.

The present partial interference of the British Government promotes the INCREASE, CELEBRITY, *and* SUPPOSED LEGALITY *of the Suttee.*

The sentiment of the Poet, "'Tis but lame kindness that does its work by halves," applies with peculiar force to the regulations enacted in British India relative to the burning of widows. This will appear by the following extracts from the Parliamentary Papers relating to Hindoo widows: No. i, ii, iii, iv,; printed July, 1821; June, 1823; June, 1824; and July, 1825.—

* Friend of India, (monthly series), Vol. ii. Page 458—483.

"It appears to me that, if the practice is allowed to exist at all, the less notice we take of it the better, because the apparent object of the interference of the police is to compel the people to observe the rules of their own shastras, (which of themselves they will not obey), by ascertaining particular circumstances of the condition of the widow. The object of the interference does not appear to answer the proposed end: for, with the same means of obtaining information, the number of widows burnt in 1817 far exceeds that in the preceding years. It is true, that the interference of the police may, in some cases, have induced compliance with the rules of the shastras; but *the official attendance of the darogah stamps every regular Suttee with the sanction of Government;* and I must humbly submit, that authorizing a practice is not the way to effect its gradual abolition."* (W. Ewer, Esq., Act. Sup. of Police, Lower Provinces, Calcutta, Nov., 1818.)

"Mr. Chapman entirely agrees with Mr. Oakley that the interference of Government has been a cause of the increased prevalence of Suttee."† (W. Ewer, Esq., &c.)

"I should not deem it improbable that the interference of the police officers, under the orders of Government, may have tended to increase the practice, by acting as a stimulus, in the same manner that the interference of European Governments with the religious tenets of any sect, has always tended to increase the zeal and confirm the prejudices of the sectaries." ‡ (J. Ewing, Esq., Magistrate, Sylhet.)

"Previous to 1813, no interference on the part of the police was authorized, and widows were sacrificed legally or illegally as it might happen; but the Hindoos were then aware that the Government regarded the custom with natural horror, and would do any thing short of direct prohibition to discourage and gradually to abolish it. The case is now altered. The police officers are ordered to interfere, for the purpose of ascertaining that the ceremony is performed in conformity with the rules of the shastras, and in that event to allow its completion. This is *granting the authority of Government for the burning of widows;* and it can scarcely be a matter of astonishment that the number of the sacrifices should be doubled when *the sanction of the ruling power is added to the recommendation of the shastra.*"§ (H. Oakley, Esq., Mag., Hooghly, Dec., 1818.)

"The Governor General in Council is reluctantly led to express his apprehension that the greater confidence with which the people perform this rite under the sanction of Government, as implied or avowed in the circular orders already in force, combined with the excitement of religious bigotry by the continual agitation of the question, may have tended to augment, rather than diminish, the frequency of these sacrifices." ‖ (Calcutta, Dec., 1819.) The increase here referred to was evident from the returns of Suttees in the several districts subordinate to the Presidency of Fort William, viz., in the year,

"1815 .... 378.
1816 .... 442.
1817 .... 707." ¶

* Par. Papers, No i. p. 229. † p. 232. ‡ p. 232. § p. 236. ‖ p. 242. ¶ p. 241.

Relative to the increase of Suttees, the Magistrates in the Allypore district remark, "The abstract statement of the number of Suttees exhibits the frequency of these abominable sacrifices so progressively and materially increased since the period referred to, (from 1815 to 1818), as to justify our being confirmed in the belief, before more than once expressed by this, to the superior Court, that any interference, save that of *a total prohibition under the severest penalties*, will ever be productive of a mistaken spirit of jealousy and opposition, which will hope by encouraging the prevalence of this superstitious usage, to induce us to discontinue altogether our interference."* (Allypore, March, 1819.)

"As far as my observation goes, I shall say that the humane intentions of the framers of the regulations regarding these ceremonies will not be fully answered. It can hardly be doubted but that the necessary presence of the police officers of Government, at these immolations, stamps on them that character of *strict legality* and seem to afford them that degree of *countenance* on the part of Government which must produce an evil effect." † (J. F. Petty, Esq., Mag., Southern Concan.)

"After having weighed, with every deliberation, the mode of carrying into effect the intention of Government, I became most fully satisfied *that if the prohibitory points to the sacrifice were to be determined by native police officers, the practice of this awful rite would shortly multiply manifold.*" ‡ (J. Marriott, Esq., Mag., Tannah, Sep. 1819.)

"Our Government, by modifying the thing and issuing orders about it,—orders which even the Government and the Sudder Judges themselves do not appear clearly to comprehend, have thrown the ideas of the Hindoos upon the subject into a complete state of confusion. They know not what is allowed and what interdicted; but, upon the whole, they have a persuasion that our Government, whom they most erroneously suppose to be indifferent about the lives of the natives, are *rather favourable to Suttees than otherwise.* They will then believe that we abhor the usage when we prohibit *in toto* by an absolute and peremptory law. They have no idea that we might not do so with the most perfect safety. *They conceive our power and our will to be commensurate.*"§ (C. Smith, Esq., Second Judge, Calcutta, Aug., 1821.)

The Hon. the Court of Directors, in a letter to the Governor General in Council, under date London, June, 1823, thus express their opinion upon the subject of partial interference,—"To us it appears very doubtful (and we are confirmed in this doubt by respectable authority) whether the measures which have been already taken have not tended rather to increase than to diminish the frequency of the practice. Such a tendency is, at least, not unnaturally ascribed to a Regulation which, *prohibiting a practice only in certain cases, appears to sanction it in all others.* It is to be apprehended, that where the people have not previously a very enthusiastic attachment to the custom, a law which shall explain to them

* Par. Papers, No. i. p. 218. † p. 254. ‡ 255, 256. § No. ii. p. 67.

the cases in which it ought not to be followed may be taken as a direction for adopting it in all others. It is, moreover, with much reluctance that we can consent to make the British Government, by a specific permission of the Suttee, *an ostensible party to the sacrifice;* we are averse also to the practice of making British Courts expounders and vindicators of the Hindoo religion, when it leads to acts which, not less as Legislators than as Christians, we abominate." *

"A general opinion prevails (in which I most cordially concur), that, in order to reduce the frequency of this rite, it should be neglected and treated with as little notice as possible." † (J. J. Sparrow, Esq., Col. & Mag., S. Concan, Feb., 1822.)

The opinions of the second, third, and fifth Judges of the Nizamut Adawlut in Calcutta, are as follows:—

"The second Judge cannot subscribe to any instructions that have a tendency to *modify, systematize, or legalize the usage,* or that appear to regard a legal Suttee as at all better than an illegal one. He is convinced, that if this mode of issuing orders under the sanction of Government to regulate Suttees is continued, *the practice will take such deep root, under the authority of the supreme power of the country, that to eradicate it will become impossible.* The usage will be much more likely to fall into disuse under a total neglect on the part of Government, than under the present system of attention and inquiry, which serves but to keep the feelings of the Hindoo population alive upon the point, and to give a sort of interest and celebrity to the sacrifice, which is in the highest degree favourable to its continuance and extension." ‡ (C. Smith, Esq.)

"I conceive that we have already done a great deal of mischief in this way, and that instead of diminishing we have increased the evil."§ (J. T. Shakespeare, Esq.)

"I confess that my own opinion inclines me to impute to the Regulations a positively pernicious tendency, in proportion to the degree in which they have brought the sacrifices under the more immediate cognizance of the officers of Government, whose presence at the ceremony, instead of operating as a restraint, has, I am afraid, contributed to invest it with additional solemnity, and to confer on the performance of it, in the mistaken view of the natives, a species of *authoritative sanction* which it was not before considered to possess."‖ (W. B. Martin, Esq.)

"It can hardly be doubted but that the printed work regarding Suttees has given the ceremony, in the eyes of the natives, *a stamp of legality which in our Provinces—it never before possessed;* and it may therefore be questioned whether, upon the whole, more harm than good may not have followed its publication." ¶ (Bombay, Jud. Cons., June, 1820.)

"This permission I found that the people most ignorantly and perversely abused; and, at every stage of my argument with them, an appeal was made to *the order of Government*, as a vindication of their conduct. There can be no doubt of the benevolent intention of Go-

---

* Par. Papers, No. iii. p. 45. † p. 48. ‡ No. iv. p. 148. § p. 149. ‖ p. 149. ¶ p. 156.

vernment in issuing such an order, and as little of its beneficial influence in many instances, as it prevents the employment of force; but, the people construe it into *a direct approval* of the dreadful act; and for a long time '*The order of Government*' seemed to form a triumphant answer to all my arguments.'" And again:—"The only answer they attempted to give was, 'It is the custom, and we have got the Government order for so doing.'"* (Extracts from Bombay Courier, Oct., 1824.

From these observations it is presumed that partial interference with the burning of Hindoo widows has not been attended with the desired end—the discountenance and decrease of Suttees; but that rather the appalling evil has increased in enormity, celebrity, and supposed legality. Humanity and justice dictate "a more excellent way," enjoining the ancient precept of the Almighty to Noah and his sons—"Whoso sheddeth man's blood, by man shall his blood be shed." (Gen. ix. 6.) May Britain "awake to righteousness," nor fear to spread the shield over the heads of the deluded and oppressed widows daily appointed to death by this unnatural and suicidal custom, and doubtless "the blessing of those who were ready to perish will come upon her, and she will cause the widow's heart to sing for joy."

SECTION VI.

Authorities to confirm the propriety and safety of the immediate suppression of Suttees.

THE papers relating to the burning of Hindoo widows, printed by order of the Hon. the House of Commons, contain numerous authorities for the immediate suppression of this *dreadful rite*. "From what I have heard of several very respectable brahmuns, I am almost satisfied that the exercise of a very trifling degree of authority would put a stop to this perversion of reason and humanity. It appears that the late *Peishwa* frequently *personally exerted himself* to dissuade women from becoming Suttees; and that he always took upon himself the charge of supporting those who attended to this advice. I shall be glad to use my influence at this place, in a similar manner, if authorized by you, and have little doubt of the success of my interposition, in the majority of cases that may occur, when I have it in my power to assure the women of the means of subsistence."†—(H. Pottinger, Esq., Collector; addressed to the Hon. M. Elphinstone, Governor of Bombay, Oct., 1818.)

"The letter from the Magistrate of Chinsurah deserves the serious attention of the Nizamut Adawlut and the Government. It appears that this abhorrent, and often utterly illegal practice, was forbidden by the foreign Governments of those settlements: and that the prohibition was obeyed without a murmur. So little do the people ap-

* Par. Papers, No. iv. p. 212, 213. † No. i. p. 65.

pear to have interested themselves in the affair, that we find, from Mr. Forbes' letter, that the mere publication of an order from himself prohibiting the practice, effectually prevented it, and that no single instance of a woman burning herself has occurred since. Women cannot burn or be burnt within the Supreme Court, and as we do not find that this prevention has excited the slightest religious alarm in Calcutta, we beg to call the attention of the Nizamut Adawlut to the fact, in proof that no necessity whatever exists why those who assist in killing women in this way should not be treated as murderers in other parts of the British territories."* (E. Watson, Esq., Allypore, April, 1816.)

"If the British, *in imitation of the Moghul Government*, were to lay an immediate and positive inhibition upon it, and would declare the parties aiding in the ceremony indictable for murder, and proceed against them accordingly, *it must totally die away;* but if tolerated, under whatever restrictions, I do not hesitate to pronounce that it will, in a short time, become nearly as prevalent as it now is in Bengal."† (W. Wright, Esq., Mag., Furruckabad, April, 1819.)

"I do not think that much, if any, difficulty would be experienced in abolishing the custom of Suttee, if a law for that purpose were to be established."‡ (W. P. Pechell, Esq., Mag., Chittagong, Dec. 18.)

"I do not hesitate in offering my opinion, that a law for its abolition would only be objected to by *the heirs*, who derive worldly profit from the custom,—by brahmuns, who partly exist by it,—and by those whose depraved nature leads them to look on a sacrifice as an highly entertaining show; at any rate the sanction of Government should be withdrawn without delay. The adoption of this measure will most likely be followed by a decrease in the number of Suttees, and the *Magistrate's feelings will not be outraged, as they frequently are at present*, by compelling him to so barbarous a custom."§ (H. Oakley, Esq., Mag., Hooghly, Dec., 1818.)

"The interference of Government is well understood to be the Christian wish of humanity. The Rajah of this place is a Mussulman; and the Hindoos seem generally willing to embrace the excuse of the will of the reigning power to evade the Suttee, believed of their little-read, and less understood shastra."‖ (R. Morrieson, Esq., Sory Burthom, Dec. 1818.)

"A law might doubtless be promulgated for the abolition of this practice, without causing any serious disturbance. It has already been done in regard to the sacrifice of children at Saugor and elsewhere, as well as the practice of destroying female infants, and the burying alive of women. Why, if these customs, which were also generally practised, have been abolished by a humane Government, should not the practice of Suttee be abolished? The destruction of a woman, or of a child, in the eye of the law, is equal; the free consent alleged in palliation of the sacrifice appears to me inadmissible; that is, no fair judgment can be passed upon a person *non compos mentis*, assenting to the performance of this act; for can a person be called actually in a sound state of mind and reason under the agitation of

* Par. Papers, No. i. p. 99, 100. † p. 212. ‡ p. 233. § p. 237. ‖ p. 238.

grief? and would a person's deposition, under this state of mind, be received in a court of justice in a case where life and death are at stake? Look at the statements; they exhibit a class of people who must have been generally ignorant of the shastras."* (E. Lee Warner, Esq., Mag., 24 Pergunnahs, Calcutta, Dec., 1818.)

C. Chapman, Esq. Magistrate in Jessore, under date Dec., 1818, thus addresses the Acting Superintendent of Police, Lower Provinces, Calcutta, relative to Suttees:—"Any law, abolishing the Suttee, would be attended with no other effect than it should have under every good system of Government—the *immediate and due observance of its enactments.* I would most willingly undertake to promulgate any orders regarding its abolition, throughout the district under my charge, without dread of any ill consequences arising from the interference of Government."†

G. Forbes, Esq., first Judge of the Calcutta Court of Circuit, thus writes to the Register of the Nazamut Adawlut, Aug., 1819:—"I take this opportunity to express my concurrence in the opinion which I found to prevail with *the judicial officers at the several stations*, with whom I conversed on the subject, that the practice of Hindoo women burning themselves on the funeral pile of their deceased husbands, if prohibited by Government, might be effectually suppressed without apprehension of any serious obstacles. I am happy in being able to adduce an instance of effectual interference in the suppression of this barbarous custom under British authority. In the territory of Delhi, the late resident, Mr. Metcalfe, *never* (when apprised of the intention) *permitted the burning of a widow to take place, and was prepared to prevent the practice, whenever necessary, by forcible interference, but which was requisite* ONLY ON ONE OCCASION *that came under his immediate observation.* I have been induced to mention the instance of successful interference by the Resident of Delhi, as affording an example which I believe nearly every Magistrate in the country would, if authorized, be most happy to follow; and in order to show that there appears no insurmountable obstacle to a measure, with regard to the exigency of which, if shown to be practicable, there can be but one sentiment."‡

F. Warden, Esq., one of the Members of Council in Bombay, thus declares his opinion:—"I am convinced of the practicability of abolishing not only *this*, but also *every other sanguinary practice of the Hindoos*, and without endangering either the popularity or the security of our supremacy."§

J. O. Tod, Esq., Judge in the Masulipatam Zilla, under the Madras Presidency, thus expresses his opinion relative to suppressing Suttees, July, 1819:—"The practice is by no means common in this part of the country; and that it might be altogether abolished by an ordinance of Government, without offence to the religious feelings or prejudices of the natives seems, not impossible from the following circumstance:—Application was once made to the criminal Judge, when he held the office of Magistrate, by the relations of a widow, for his permission to burn herself with the dead body of her husband. He

* Par. Papers, No. i. p. 239. † p. 241. ‡ p. 243. § p. 261.

informed them that the British Government made it a rule never to interfere with the religious prejudices or customs of the natives, and that therefore he would not give any order whatever to the woman *herself*, who might act as she should think became her; but he assured them that he would immediately commit, *as accomplices in the murder*, all persons who should in any way assist her to destroy herself, and the consequence was, that the woman did not burn, but is alive and well at this day. This measure did not cause the least dissatisfaction, on the contrary, the relations of the woman appeared pleased at her having obtained a decent pretext for avoiding the horrid ceremony.*

The Parliamentary Papers, No. iii, printed June, 1824, contain little beside a detail of the number, names, casts, &c. of Suttees in 1821. The following expression of public opinion relative to the abolition of the burning of widows, appears important:—

"As far as every information I can obtain, this revolting ceremony could be altogether prevented, by a short prohibitory enactment of the Legislature."† (R. C. Plowden, Esq., Barripore, June, 1822, to C. H. Hopper, Esq. Mag., of the 24 Pergunnahs, Calcutta.)

Inquiry having been made by the Superintendent of Police, Madras, relative to a woman desirous of burning herself, though dissuaded by her relatives, yet those relations, upon her persisting in her intentions, desiring she should be permitted to do so, received the following reply from the Secretary of Government, dated Fort St. George, March 7, 1823:—"I am directed to acknowledge the receipt of your letter of yesterday's date, and to express the opinion of the Hon. the Governor in Council, that all practicable means should be employed for preventing the woman in question from making the intended sacrifice of herself. With that view, her relations should be informed, that *such a practice being contrary to the established usage of this place, cannot obtain the sanction of Government*, and that it is considered to be their duty to use their strongest persuasions and influence to induce her to forego her intentions. You will also apprize them that they will be held answerable for any interference of a contrary tendency."‡

The success attending efforts to discountenance the perpetration of Suttees under the Presidencies of Madras and Bombay have been attended with great encouragement, and shew the fecility of entirely suppressing this *unnatural and murderous rite*. According to the returns of Suttees for the Madras Presidency, from 1817 to 1819, the number was 183; from 1821—1823 no returns, average per annum sixty-one.

Under the Bombay Presidency, from 1819 to 1823, 245, average per annum 49. Who can doubt whether these few individuals sacrificed every year could not be saved in those extensive territories without exciting the least commotion! Nor is the evil under the Bengal Presidency (containing probably a population of 50,000,000,) so great as to deter exertions for its suppression, the number of Suttees being, from

* Par. Papers, No. ii. p. 85. † No. iii. p. 4. ‡ p. 51.

1819—1821, 3059, average per annum 611.* Might not British humanity, magnanimity, and piety, rescue these without the least danger to the state? The multitude of counsellors reply in the affirmative.

The nature of the system of discountenancing Suttees pursued on the Madras side of India is as follows:—"Where, (says the writer of the following article, in a Calcutta paper), the immolation of widows *though once frequent, is now seldom known.*"

"Before any woman can destroy herself by burning, permission must first be obtained from the Magistrate. On the request being referred, the applicant is directed to wait a little for an answer; the Magistrate in the mean time sends for his Cutwal and instructs him to proclaim that a certain widow intends burning herself, but should any Bunian or Bukall be discovered selling any article required for the purpose to the said woman, or any cooly (labourer) offering his assistance by carrying oil, wood, &c. to the spot appointed, the former shall be turned out of the bazar, and the latter otherwise punished. It is also proclaimed, that should any crowd collect, the police peons are constantly to disperse it, and to confine to the Cutwal's Choultry all persons resisting the police authority; further, should any brahmun belonging to the public offices be seen in the crowd, or any of his relations be found aiding and abetting in the ceremony, *such servant shall be discharged from his situation.* The whole of this being proclaimed, the applicant is desired to take leave. As may be expected it has been observed, that *with these restrictions no burning has taken place!* The prevailing practice therefore with us may be said to be a complete remedy, and points out that a remedy exists for the prevention of so material an evil. It is briefly this—*prevent a crowd from collecting to witness the immolation, and rest assured no such ceremony proceeds!* Mark the disappointment of the brahmun when he discovers that a crowd (for what is a Hindoo ceremony or feast without a concourse of people!) cannot be collected; mortified, he abandons the victim of his persuasion to shift for herself. His zeal is exerted in proportion to his expected popularity, or to the worldly advantage he is to derive. So it is with the poor deluded widows, harrassed and goaded into assent to they know not what; ninety-nine out of a hundred of them secretly rejoice that their attempt at self-destruction has been, by the above means, frustrated. As the remedy can hardly be said to be attended with coercion, it appears no difficult undertaking to introduce the practice of it in Bengal, and hereby render an essential service to the Hindoo community." (R. S. Moligaipore, March, 1823.)

J. H. Harington, Esq., officiating Chief Judge in Calcutta, in a minute relative to the Suttee of considerable length and interest, dated June, 1823, gives much information upon the subject before us. This document was forwarded to the Court of Directors by the Governor-General, Dec., 1824. See Par. Papers, No. iii, printed July, 1825, p. 8—18. A few extracts cannot but be interesting:—

"I am desirous of putting upon record some considerations which appear to merit attention in any future deliberation upon this import-

* See Account of the York Meeting for the Suppression of Suttees, p. 21.

ant question, and which, I acknowledge, have produced in my own mind a strong belief, if not a full conviction, that whenever it may be judged expedient to suppress this barbarous practice by legal prohibition, instead of restricting it to what is sanctioned by the shastra, as at present, *it will not be found impracticable*, *or*, *as far as I can judge*, *be attended with any serious political danger.* It is probable that a proclamation to this effect (abolishing the practice) would not at once prove completely effectual; secret immolations would still take place occasionally, and in some instances the widow, under a paroxysm of grief, and the delusion of superstition, might be expected to devote herself on her husband's funeral pile, or otherwise, even without brahminical assistance; but such cases would be rare in comparison with the number of sacrifices which now take place annually, either with or without the knowledge of the police officers; and after a few examples for wilful deviation from the rule newly promulgated, (which should of course be made with tenderness in the early infliction of penalties,) *I have no doubt that the practice would be soon abandoned as unsanctioned by Government, and subjecting the aiders and abettors to punishment by the criminal Courts.* On a deliberate view of all those instances in which the laws, customs, and prejudices of the Hndoos, when found to be at variance with the principles of justice and good society, have been necessarily superseded and abrogated by the laws and regulations of the British Government,* and in the whole of which such supercession has been quietly submitted to, *as obviously and exclusively originating in motives of equity and humanity, unconnected with any degree of religious intolerance*, we may, I think, safely conclude that a similar result will attend the enactment of a legislative provision to prevent the yearly sacrifice of several hundreds of deluded unoffending females, born and living under the protection of the British Government, whenever it shall be deemed expedient to make and promulgate the requisite enactment for that purpose."

This interesting document thus closes. Referring to certain probable excesses in the perpetration of Suttees, it is added, "In such a state of things I could not hesitate to adopt the opinion expressed by the second Judge of the Court of Nizamut Adawlut, that the toleration of the practice of Suttees is a reproach to our Government; and *even now* I am disposed to agree with him, '*that the entire and immediate abolition of it would be attended with no sort of danger.*'"

Among the papers forwarded to the Hon. Court of Directors was one containing, says Mr. Harington, "an extract from a well-written paper, 'On *female immolation*,' published in the valuable periodical work, entitled '*The Friend of India*,'† which the late Sir Henry Blossett and myself read on our voyage to India, and which appeared to

---

* Such as the execution of brahmuns: suppressing the sacrifice of children at Saugur; preventing women and children, in the provinces of Benares, from burning in a *koorh*, or circular inclosure, on the approach of a public officer to serve any judicial process on brahmuns; abolishing Dhurna, infanticide among the Rajkoomars, &c.—*See Asiatic Researches*, *Vol.* iv. *p.* 330.

† See Friend of India, (quar. ser.) No. iii. March, 1821.

both of us a powerful and convincing statement of the real facts and circumstances of the case."* A few passages from it may be interesting:—

"We are confident that the continuance of the practice stands on the doctrine of *expediency alone.* This is its only prop; of which could it once be deprived it would fall beneath the weight of justice and humanity. And considering the British supremacy in the East as the greatest blessing which the natives have yet received, it does become a duty to look forward to remote consequences which may attend any act of benevolence. The Government of this country has done much to alleviate the misery of India, and to counteract the mischief of its native depravity; and were it practicable with one stroke of the pen to remove every misery, and diffuse happiness through the country, we are sure it would not be withheld for a moment. It cannot therefore be improper to weigh the question of expediency, and to collect into one focus all the light which can be obtained on the subject from our preceding transactions in India. And if it should thence appear that we have not hitherto been arrested in our career of justice by the prejudices of the natives, that on the contrary the Hindoos have already gone hand in hand with us, without discovering any hostility to our authority. There can be no reason to apprehend that, in the abolition of female immolation, we shall experience the least interruption. To prove that this is the case, we will adduce three examples:—

"In the province of Guzerat the deluded parents had been for a long series of years in the habit of destroying their female infants as soon as they were born. Whether the custom was sanctioned by the shastras or not, is irrevelent; it is enough that it was deeply rooted in the practice and prejudices of the natives. These unnatural murders at length attracted the attention of Government, and *they were abolished by an order of the supreme power.* Did Government immediately lose the confidence and attachment of the natives? Did the enraged parent, unsheathing his sword, slaughter the reserved victim, and then turn it on those who had attempted its preservation? Not one symptom of disaffection has been manifested by the natives on this account. By some the practice is probably forgotten; and it would now appear in the eyes of those as horrible as it formerly appeared natural and indispensable.

"Our second example is of the same nature, but as it indicates the feelings of a class of natives at the other extremity of the continent, in the opinion of some it may carry greater weight, as demonstrating that the same security accompanies every assertion of the principles of humanity throughout this vast empire. From time immemorial it was the custom of mothers to sacrifice their children to the Ganges at the annual festival held at Gunga Saugur. The British Government regarded the practice with those feelings of horror which such unnatural murders are calculated to inspire; as persuasion would have been unavailing with those who had parted with every parental feeling, *the practice was prohibited by a public regulation, and the pro-*

* Par. Papers, No. iv. p. 13.

hibition enforced by public authority. Nor let us forget that this order was promulgated in the presence of thousands assembled at a public festival, in the highest excitement of superstitious frenzy. What was the consequence? Not one instance of resistance was attempted by that immense crowd—the mischief vanished from the earth, and no one bewailed it! The mothers who had brought their children to this funeral sacrifice were constrained to carry them back unhurt; and many, perhaps to whom the heinousness of the crime had never appeared, were, by this interposition, awakened to a sense of its enormity!

"The third example will perhaps go farther to show that we have pursued a course of undeviating justice in India, at the expense of religious injunction and popular prejudice. The Hindoo laws absolutely prohibit the execution of a brahmun; they forbid the Magistrate even to imagine evil against him. Thus fenced by the laws, and extolled by their sacred books, they are still more powerfully guarded by the respect and veneration of the people. From one corner of India to the other, however, religious observances may have fallen into disuse, this sacred tribe enjoys great homage. When therefore our Government commenced in the East we were reduced to the most serious dilemma. To have inflicted punishment on brahmuns would have been to violate the most awful sanctions of Hindoo law, and the dearest prejudices of the people; to have exempted them from punishment would have been to deliver over the country to desolation, ravage, and murder. The reign of equity which we were about to introduce was stopped at the very threshold; the destiny of millions hung in suspense. How did we act on this occasion? Did we lay the laws of justice at the feet of the sacred tribe? Did we abrogate our code of jurisprudence, and adopt the Vedas for our guide? Did we deprive the country of our protection because the Hindoo shastras forbid the punishment of the aggressors, if they happen to be brahmuns? We did not hesitate a single moment, but boldly stepped forward in vindication of the rights of society; and in spite of a formidable phalanx of Hindoo juris-consults, and of the strongest prejudices, caused these delinquents to pay the forfeit of their lives to the laws of offended justice. We have repeated the punishment of brahmuns since that period whenever it has been requisite; and scarcely a year has since elapsed without the execution of a brahmun in some one of the provinces of our empire. Have the natives complained of this outrage on the sanctity of their priesthood, or considered it as an infringement of our toleration? Have we lost their confidence? Have they, in any one instance, petitioned us to disregard their welfare and exempt their spiritual guides from death? or have they not on the contrary tacitly sanctioned every act of punishment, and applauded the inflexible tenor of our proceedings? Let any man read the account of Nundkomar's execution in Calcutta, forty years ago, and he will be convinced that Hindoos are not men to complain of *the execution of justice, even though it happen to infringe their laws and prejudices.* Mr. Hastings judged there could be no danger in his execution; and his judgment proved correct. If ever it might have been expected that public feeling would have manifested itself against us, it was most assuredly in this instance, when, for the first time, we were carrying the law into execution against one of this sacred tribe; where the actors in this unprecedented exhibition of justice were but a handful compared with the immense crowd (full 200,000 of his own countrymen!) which surrounded the scaffold; that vast crowd returned peaceably to their houses. If Mr. Hasting's intrepid support of the claims of justice, in the face of such formidable obstacles, should continue to encourage others, and thereby prove a lasting benefit to the natives of India, more solid glory will inscribe his memory than as though we covered the plains of India with obelisks."*

In reviewing the annual statement of Suttees, in the Zillahs and Cities of India presented to the Government, while it is distressing to see with what *frequency, indifference, and brutality*, the unhappy widow is hurried out of the world, it is grateful to see humanity sometimes triumph, and the infatuated victim rescued; affording demonstration how easily

> "*One mild effort* of the conquering hand
> Might free the earth from this detested blot,
> And lead in blest religion to withstand
> By her meek precepts, what has dimm'd the lot
> Of man, and wrought such deeds as cannot be forgot."

In the Bareilly Division it is reported, that in 1815 three women were prevented becoming Suttees. In the Patna Division, in 1817, twenty-five Suttees took place, but five women were prevented who "were saved from burning by the interference of the people of the village or by the arrival of the police officers." In the same year five Suttees are stated to have been prevented in the City of Benares. In the following year three other Suttees were prevented in the same City, and "one woman, cast a brahmun, ran away from the pile after it was set fire to, and is still living." Four widows were saved at Cuddapah in 1820.†

The Magistrate of the Patna Division, in his returns of Suttees for 1822, writes,—"It is with satisfaction that I have noted, at the foot of the report, that TWELVE WIDOWS have been either prevented or dissuaded from becoming Suttees; in nine of which they were dissuaded by the police officers; in one the widow was prevented by a police officer on account of a legal impediment, and in the two remaining cases the widows were dissuaded, in one by the Zemindar of the village, and in the other by her friends. A police officer was present in only one of the numerous cases in which the sacrifice was completed (and in that he should have prevented it!) although, as it may be observed, many of the villages in which they took place are not far from the police stations."

In the returns from the same Division of the following year (1823) are the following highly interesting statements:—"It will probably be considered the most remarkable feature of the present report that, on *nine occasions* of intended Suttee, at which alone the police officers

* Par. Papers, No. iv. p. 22—24.—Friend of India, as above.
† Par. Papers, printed July, 1821, and June, 1823

had an opportunity of being present, they succeeded, without difficulty or opposition, in dissuading the widows from sacrificing themselves. From the inquiries that I have been able to make on the subject of Suttees during the last two years, I do not hesitate to offer an opinion, that in this district it would not be attended with any dissatisfaction of a dangerous nature, if the Government should deem it proper, *to prohibit this lamentable custom altogether;* it even appears to me that the inhabitants of the district generally are prepared to hear of such a prohibition." Oh! when shall suffering humanity in India hear the voice of mercy saying, "kindle those horrid fires no more! In some parts of Orissa a pit is used for this dreadful sacrifice, and the woman, after circumambulating it three or seven times, throws herself into the fire. I have seen one of these pits at Juggernaut's temple, but did not hear of the Suttee in time to be present. Even from this pit the Suttee sometimes escapes. In the Par. Papers (printed July, 1825, p. 109 and 150) is the following account:—"Rahang in the Thannah, of Pooree, (Juggernaut) died Aug., 25, 1823, and his widow, Mussumut Munee, aged 50, declared her intentions of becoming a Suttee, and repeated the declaration in presence of the police officers. In pursuance of this intention, the day following she went through the usual ceremonies, and *threw herself into a burning pit, where the body of her husband was consuming*, but almost immediately leapt out and made her escape. She was severely, but not dangerously burnt, and an engagement was taken from the managers of the village binding themselves that she should be taken care of and proper remedies applied. She returned to her family, and was received by them as usual."

Private friendship prompts me to record here the rescue of a poor woman from the flaming pit at Pooree, and this event, like the preceding, shews, "while rescuing one, how practicable it is, with ease, to rescue all." The account is contained in the Report of the General Baptist Missionary Society for 1826, and is as follows:—

"On Friday, Oct. 28, 1825, we were informed that there would be a Suttee in the afternoon. Brother B. wrote to the different Europeans at the stations, thinking that some from motives of curiosity or humanity might wish to attend, but no hope could be entertained of saving the poor woman, as we were told that she had already burnt her fingers in order to prove her fortitude. Brother B. declined going, having seen one Suttee, and being so disgusted at the horrid scene;—and from what he then saw, and did, feeling persuaded that it was in vain to attempt to save the wretched victim, he despaired of doing any good. I however felt a desire to witness the horrid work, that I might speak from experience; and two military gentlemen having expressed their determination to go, at about half-past four we set off towards the spot where the Suttee was to take place: the name of the place is Swergo Dwar, or The Gate of Heaven; a place thickly strewed with human skulls and skeletons of Juggernaut's adorers. About a furlong from the pit we ascertained, from the noise of the tin kettle-drums, &c., that the woman was approaching. In a few minutes a vast concourse of people made their appearance, shouting and beating their drums, &c.; even little children were employed in this unholy work. In the centre of a crowd we discerned the destined victim, surrounded by a slight hoop of bamboo, so that she might walk clear from the press. She appeared to be under twenty years of age, and of an interesting appearance. Round her person was wrapped a white cloth smeared with turmeric; under her right arm she carried a handy, or earthen pot, containing a little rice, a piece of cocoa-nut, one or two other trifling things, and some fire to throw into the pit, this was from Juggernaut's temple: in her left hand she held some pice (halfpence) which she was to distribute to the bystanders. Her jet-black hair was smeared with ghee and other greasy substances, and decorated with flowers and gaudy ornamented paper: round her neck was a large rope nearly as thick as my wrist, and one or two smaller ones: thus attired, she looked the picture of all that is degraded and wretched. Before her stood one of Satan's high priests with two paltry pictures of Juggernaut, which he was very anxious she should look upon continually. Altogether, I never saw any thing so infernal. The barbarous indifference of the multitude to every feeling of humanity—the thoughts of an awful eternity—the idea that the poor creature before me would soon rush, thus polluted with Idolatry, into the presence of an awful God, who hates sin and abominates Idolatry—the multitude who evinced so savage a pleasure in the bloody work—and the malicious countenances of the principal actors in this wretched scene, rendered more horrible than ever by the interruption, altogether so pressed upon my mind that the feeling beggars description. But what could be done! something must be attempted. We bid the people stop. I got off my horse, and the two Europeans came near with their elephant; I made my way to the woman, and found she was quite intoxicated; there was a strange wildness in her appearance. I looked at her eyes, turned up the eyelids and found them very bloodshot and heavy: the woman could not utter a syllable distinctly, all that could be understood was, 'Juggernaut,' and 'koosee,' meaning, I suppose, Juggernaut is my pleasure. A thrill of horror ran through my veins: her youth—her destitute condition, for she had not a friend even to 'give her fire,' viz., light the pile—her total insensibility—and the general horror of the scene, induced the mutual feeling that she was about to be cruelly murdered. We thought the law protected us under such circumstances, and determined to rescue her. The people looked at us amazed; the crowd soon thickened upon us, and assumed rather a formidable appearance; but there was no time for parley, we put on a determined aspect, and insisted on her being taken back, urging that she was quite intoxicated: this many of them admitted, but still retained their hold of the hoop by which she was enclosed, and urged that it was her wish to burn, and that it was Juggernaut's pleasure; we however insisted upon her being taken back till she was sensible. Captain G. and Lieutenant M. behaved nobly, they charged a few servants in their employ to keep off the people; they soon gave way without making any further resistance, and left us in charge of the woman and the principal actors. I should observe that the Daroga (head police-officer) was absent. I then mounted my horse and rode before, the road was made through the crowd by the servants and a few idle seapoys who attended as lookers on, the officers followed the woman on their elephant till they saw all was safe, and then returned to the pile. I rode before the crowd and the woman towards the police officer's place of confinement: in my way I met with brother B. and surprised him with what was done: he accompanied me to the prison, and delivered the woman into the charge of the Daroga, who was much surprised and disconcerted at what was done, but was obliged to attend to Captain G.'s orders to secure the woman. All seemed consternation. I am sure that I wondered at our success, Bampton seemed to wonder more; the people seemed thunderstruck, and exclaimed, 'Now you have done something!' others said, 'This is merciful!' and indeed among the thousands of spectators not a sound of disapprobation was heard, or the least confusion excited. The woman herself kept saying, as well as we could understand, 'This is well done! you have broken my purposes:' she was however quite stupified. What may be the result we know not, or whether we shall be able to save her is quite uncertain; we know, however, it might be done with the most trifling interference on the part of the Magistrate. Her husband's corpse is already consumed."

He adds,—"On Tuesday the Judge, much to his credit and honour, determined that the woman *should not burn*. May God overrule it to promote his own glory, and for the putting out for ever these flames which hell itself has kindled. O that this circumstance may be the harbinger of this happy consummation! How easily might it be done! Only think, that three individuals, at the very worst place in all India, without authority, and without the least disturbance, and without giving offence to any except three or four individuals immediately concerned, have succeeded in saving this wretched woman from the devouring flames!"

If so much satisfaction is felt by humane minds in the rescue of a single individual, how would humanity—how would Christianity hail the merciful suppression of all those barbarities!

The opinion of J. H. Harington, Esq, officiating chief Judge in the Nizamut Adawlut, Calcutta, relative to the expediency of abolishing the Suttee, has been given. The second Judge, C. Smith, Esq., says: —"The practice of Suttee OUGHT TO BE ABOLISHED, and it may be abolished with PERFECT SAFETY." The third Judge, J. T. Shakespear, Esq., likewise states:—"I am prepared to concur in a recommendation to Government, that a regulation be promulgated prohibiting Suttees throughout the country." The fifth Judge, W. B. Martin, Esq., at the same time stated:—"The toleration of the practice by our Government, and its disposition to interfere no further than was necessary to guard it from abuse, has been misconstrued into a tacit recognition of the principle of an usage, the legality of which within certain limits, it has formerly acknowledged."

The minute of the officiating Judge, J. Ahmuty, Esq., relative the documents from which the above extracts are taken, is as follows: —"I feel satisfied that it would be far preferable to enact a regulation *prohibiting the practice of Suttees at once, and rendering it punishable by law*, than having recourse to any partial or indirect means to repress it gradually, if even such a result could be reasonably expected to ensue."*

The Governor General in Council, Lord Amherst, evidently anticipates the final abolition of Suttee, as appears from the observations upon the statement of the number of widows who were burned in 1823. His words are:—"His Lordship in Council is unwilling to abandon the hope, that the abolition of the practice may, at a future period, be found safe and expedient; and he has already had occasion to remark, that the more general dissemination of knowledge and the discussions of the question among the better informed Hindoos themselves, may be expected to have some effect in gradually preparing the minds of the natives for such a measure.† (Jud. Depart., Dec., 1824.)

Humanity, in her tears, asks, why delay to rescue the unhappy widow? "The argument that we may ultimately look for the cure of this evil in the gradual increase of intelligence which is beginning to develope itself in India, might have some weight, if the progress of intelligence were of a more accelerated character than circumstances allow us to suppose, or if the immediate abolition of the rite were not proved to be both safe and practicable. But this fact, once satisfactorily established, to delay the enjoyment of an acknowledged good, because at some future, yet more remote time, you anticipate its attainment by the operation of other causes,—what is this but to procrastinate a happiness already within your reach, and to be justly responsible for all the misery of the intervening period of a long and criminal delay?"‡

The authorities for the propriety and safety of the immediate abolition of Suttee are numerous and decisive. This has appeared from the various references which have been made to the Parliamentary Papers upon the subject, and they may be increased from various other sources.

The Magistrate of Poona, under the Bombay Presidency, (Captain

---

* Par. Papers, No. iv. p. 148, 149. † Page 153.

‡ See Grimshawe's Appeal to British Humanity in behalf of Hindoo widows, p. 26—28.

H. D. Robertson,) thus states the nature of the popular feeling relative to Suttees:—"The feeling, I might almost say, *is general to stop them;* it was hinted to me, through various respectable channels, that although a show of discontent would be exhibited, an order of Government to prevent their continuance would be a palatable measure."*

Another Magistrate in Bombay, (J. Barnard, Esq.,) declares:—"The circumstances under which Suttees prevail, the classes interested therein, the number of instances, and the conduct of the community in their communications, both with the Magistrate and with each other, on such occasions, as well as the impressions generally entertained by those not concerned, convince me that there are few cases in which *evil would ensue from prohibition and coercive prevention.*"†

Colonel Dow, in his History of Hindoostan, says,—"All religions must be tolerated in Bengal except the practice of *some inhuman customs which the Mahomedans have already, in a great measure, destroyed.* There are particular usages, established by time into a law, which *our humanity must destroy.* Let no women burn themselves with their husbands, no dying person being exposed by his friends. To leave the natives entirely to their own laws would be to consign them to anarchy and confusion."‡ Vol. iii. p. 128, 143.

"The Commentaries of Bras de Albuquerque, the son of the Great Albuquerque, one of those extraordinary men who, nearly three hundred years ago, raised to the highest pitch of glory the Portuguese name in India, contains the following passage:—"When Alf. de Albuquerque took the kingdom of Goa he would not permit that any woman from thence forward should burn herself; and although to change their custom is equal to death, nevertheless they rejoiced in life, and said great good of him, because he commanded that they should not burn themselves. Long after his death, when a Moor or Hindoo had received wrong and could obtain no redress from the Governor, the aggrieved person would go to Goa, to Albuquerque's tomb, and make an offering of oil at the lamp which burned before it, and call upon him for justice."§ Wilberforce's Speech, 1813, 8vo. page 93, 94.

The Rev. T. S. Grimshawe, in his valuable pamphlet, called, "An earnest Appeal to British Humanity in behalf of Hindoo Widows," (1825, published by Hatchard, London,) refers to the suppression of Suttees by other powers.—

"The Mogul Government has uniformly discountenanced the practice of burning widows alive; and the extent of the benefits thus conferred may be estimated by the remarkable fact that in no part of Hindoostan is the rite *less known* than under their sway; and in none is it *more common* than in that which is the centre of British power and ascendancy! This example was humanely followed by the Portuguese. The Dutch, the Danish, and the French Governments, uniformly refused to sanction the custom. Why is the name of Bri-

* Par. Papers, No. iv. p. 167. † Page 209. ‡ "Collection of Facts and Opinions relative to the Burning of Hindoo Widows," by Dr. Johns, p. 89. § Page 103, 104.

tain alone excluded from the honourable list of competitors? Is it that policy and duty in our case are irreconcileable, however blended in that of others? The conviction is most humiliating that *the British Government is the only European power in India that tolerates the practice of burning widows alive on the funeral pile!!*" Page 16, 17.

To the same effect is the following brief extract from the article in "The Friend of India," No. iii. (quar. ser.) before noticed.—"The Mosulmans who never protected the unhappy natives from foreign invasion, or from internal commotion, checked this practice in many cases, and in some provinces abolished it altogether. Will it be too much for us while we dispense blessings with one hand, with the other to snatch the helpless victim from the flames? There is no instance on historic record in which acts of humanity have ever roused public indignation. Massacre, confiscation, and injustice are the elements from which revolutions are created, not humanity, justice, and equity; the mere supposition is a novelty in political science."*

In "An Account of the York Meeting to petition Parliament for the abolition of the immolation of Hindoo widows in British India," the reader may be furnished with much information upon the subject under consideration. In the preface of this pamphlet is the following statement relative to the views of the late Marquis of Hastings, Governor-General of India, on the abolition of Suttees:—"The importance of petitioning Parliament will be duly appreciated when it is understood that the late Marquis of Hastings said, he would at once have put down the atrocious practice, if he could have relied upon the popular feeling being in his favour in our own country, and that *the danger was felt not in India, but only in England!!*"—O when shall every town and city in Britain and Ireland say, "This blood shall not rest on us! Let no more widows perish!" Before the Marquis left India, in 1823, the following "*Supplicatory Lines*" were addressed to him in the public Papers:—

"Ere thy benignant power retires
From India, bless'd beneath thy care,
O quench these foul unhallow'd fires,
Which hell's own flame has kindled there,
The stain of earth and upper air!
Then o'er the sea,
The orphan's blessing and the widow's prayer
Shall follow thee.
O ne'er to man has pitying Heaven
A power so blest, so glorious given,
Say but a single word and save
Ten thousand mothers from a flaming grave,
And tens of thousands from the source of woe,
That ever must to orphan'd children flow!
Save from the flame the infant's place of rest,
The couch by nature given—a mother's breast;
O bid the mother live—the babe caress her,
And sweeter still its hoping accents bless her.
India with tearful eye and bended knee,
Hastings, her lord and judge, presents her plaint to thee."

Britain speak. "Plead for the widow!" Let petitions pour into Parliament from every quarter, which, like the streams of the sanc-

* Par. Papers, No. iv. p. 24—26.

tuary, shall quench these fires that hell hath kindled. Let the friends to India, who hold its destinies in their hands, hear the appeal of a writer in that country:—"Let us freely look at the practicability of its abolition, and number both its friends and its foes. We may calculate on the support of all the humane, the wise, and the good, throughout India! we may depend on the great majority of the people who have prevented every village in India from being lighted up monthly with these infernal fires. Those who used all their power and influence to liberate their country from the stigma of this guilt, by preventing their mothers and sisters from ascending the funeral pile, will undoubtedly support us in discountenancing the practice elsewhere. We shall enlist on our side all those tender feelings which, though now dormant, will then be aroused into new life and vigour; but above all we shall surround ourselves with the protection of that Almighty Power, whose command is, 'Thou shalt do no murder;' who defends the weak and succours the injured; who, when the cries of oppressed India had pierced His throne, selected us of all other nations to break its chains and restore it to happiness."*

SECTION VII.

A collection of European and Native testimony to the position that the Suttee is not absolutely enjoined by the Hindoo Shastras, and hence should be suppressed.

Menu, in his Institutes, is the great authority in determining the legality of the Suttee. Of this work Sir W. Jones, in his preface to the translation of it, says:—"This system of duties, religious and civil, and of law in all its branches, the Hindoos firmly believe to have been promulgated in the beginning of time by Menu, son or grandson of Brahma, or in plain language, the first of created beings, and not the oldest only, but the holiest of legislators." His high character is thus described in the beginning of the work:—"Menu sat reclined, with his attention fixed on one object, the supreme God; when the divine sages approached him, and after mutual salutations in due form, delivered the following address, 'Deign, sovreign ruler, to apprize us of the sacred laws in their order, as they must be followed by all the classes, and by each of them, in their several degrees, together with the duties of every mixed class; for thou, lord, and thou only among mortals, knowest the true sense, the first principle, and the prescribed ceremonies, of this universal, supernatural Veda, unlimited in extent, and unequalled in authority.'"

After a careful perusal of this work, while this pamphlet has been in the press, not the slightest reference to the horrid custom of the Suttee has been found. It contains various laws relative to women; a few extracts, in addition to what has been already quoted, may be interesting:—"In his passage to the next world, neither his father, nor his

* Par. Papers, p. 26.

mother, *nor his wife*, nor his son, nor his kinsmen, will remain in his company: his virtue alone will adhere to him. When he leaves his corse, like a log or a lump of clay, on the ground, his kindred retire with averted faces: but his virtue accompanies his soul. Equal care must be taken of women without sons, of women without kindred, of *widows* true to their lords, &c. A widow who, from a wish to bear children, slights her deceased husband, by marrying again, brings disgrace on herself here below, and shall be excluded from the seat of her lord. Like those abstemious men (unmarried brahmuns) a virtuous wife ascends to heaven, though she have no child, if, after the decease of her lord, she devote herself to pious austerity."* The duty of Hindoo widows is evidently a life of austere devotion till death, and the custom of Suttee is altogether unknown in the Institutes of the great Indian legislator.

The following extracts from the Parliamentary Papers, shewing that the Suttee is not positively enjoined, and should be suppressed, according to the opinion of many Europeans high in office in India, appear very important.—

"We really think there is as little justification for a woman to burn herself with the remains of her deceased husband, as for a ranjkoomor to destroy his daughters at their birth; burying alive for the leprosy where the party is desirous to die; human sacrifices at Saugor; putting sorcerers to death, or killing a human creature by any other means, without justification or excuse: *all of which are made capital offences by the Regulations.* The killing in all these instances has quite as much in its favour, (on the score of erroneous prejudice and superstition, and perhaps of religion), as the practice of Suttee: but we do not find the punishment of death denounced against these crimes, has at all been considered by the people as an infringement of that complete toleration, in matters of religion, which it has been a fundamental principle of the British Government to allow. *And there can be no doubt that the practice of Suttee might be as easily checked and prevented throughout the British Territories as any of the murderous practices above referred to.* We have the fact, that its suppression at the foreign Settlements was effected without the slightest difficulty."† (E. Watson, Esq., Judge, Allypore, April, 1818).

"On the subject of anoojumun (burning after the husband's death), the shastras exhibit a great variety of opinions; but *no difference prevails with regard to the propriety of leading a life of austerity.* From the above it would appear, that not the slightest offence attaches either to the women who depart from their resolution, or to those who persuade them to relinquish their intention."‡ (W. H. Macnaghten, Esq., Trans. of Mutoonjoy's Bewasta relative to Suttees, &c.)

"The suicide in these cases is not indeed a religious act, nor *has it the sanction of Menu and other ancient legislators revered by the Hindoos.* On the contrary, Menu declares that a virtuous wife ascends to heaven, though she have no child, if after the decease of her lord she devote herself to pious austerity.§ The texts of Yama and Caty-

* Sir W. Jones' Works, Vol. vii. p. 240, 334, 271. † Papers, N. i. p. 99.
‡ p. 124, 125. § Text 141; "Digest of Hindoo Law," book 4, ch. 3, sec. 2.

ayana, quoted in the *Vivada Bhangarnana* (digest of Hindoo law), "On the duties of widows choosing to survive their husbands" are also to the same effect;* and Vrihaspate adds† "whether she ascends the pile, or survive for the benefit of her husband, she is a faithful wife." Some authors have condemned the suicide of widows altogether, as coming within a general prohibition against the wilful abridgment of human life: and proceeding from a desire of future sensual enjoyment, in preference to the more pure and perfect state of beatitude promised for a life of virtue and piety." ‡ (Govt. Regulations relative to Suttees). Referring to these Regulations it is remarked:—"It is trusted they will have a very beneficial influence, by lessening a sense of obligation under which there is reason to believe many are induced to make this sacrifice of their lives, and showing that *the practice is far from being inculcated as such by the most approved authorities of the Hindoo law.*"§ (J. Adam, Esq., Sec. to the Governor General, Oct., 1817.

"I submit that *it has little or no connexion with their religion!* The practice is strongly recommended by the shastras, but nothing more, and Menu (together with other authorities of great respectability,) prescribes the duties of a widow, without *hinting* that burning herself is one of the most important. In permitting, or indeed *authorizing* Suttees, we are by no means showing a proper forbearance towards the religious customs, or long established prejudices of the Hindoos; *an act no where enjoined by any of the shastras;* on the contrary a crime which their own laws would punish with death; and only tolerated by our Government because we overlook the impudent imposition which has transformed a *recommendation* to the widow to accompany her husband, into *an order*, which the relations must carry into effect if she should evince symptoms of disobedience. I cannot attempt to account for the great prevaleuce of Suttees in some districts and the rarity of them in others; but it is a proof that it is a custom seldom thought of in the greater proportion of our dominions."‖ (W. Ewer, Esq., Act. Sup. of Police, Lower Provinces, Calcutta, Nov., 1818.) "Menu and the most ancient and respectable writers *do not mention Suttee:* it was therefore in their time either unknown or not approved. If known, but not mentioned, because not approved by Menu, the authority of the modern shastra is not sufficient to give any merit to the sacrifice. In the first case we do not find that *the practice originates in law, but the law is the consequence of the practice.* Sacred authority is subsequently produced to enforce the merit of enacting or originating on the mortal feelings of affection, grief, despair, or some other passion of the mind equally incapable of affording a hope that it could be acceptable in the eyes of the Deity."¶ (W. Ewer, Esq., as above, Calcutta, Jan., 1819.)

"After having attended at several Suttees, for the purpose of gaining as much information as possible on the subject, and after having attentively considered the doctrines under which it is sanctioned, the circumstances attending the actual performance of the sacrifice,

* Texts, 144, 145, "Digest of Hindoo Law." † Text 130. ‡ p. 126. § p. 147. ‖ p. 228. ¶ p. 231.

and the terms upon which those who have been prevented from burning have subsequently lived with their relations and neighbours, I am decidedly of opinion that *the abolition of the practice by law would not be attended with any evil consequences:* on the contrary I think the enactment of such a law is dictated by every principle of humanity; nor does it appear to me that the abolition of the practice is altogether inconsistent with the spirit of toleration which has ever distinguished the British Government. The greater proportion of the men are unable to give a reason for the performance of the sacrifice, and it is surely fair to infer that the women are not better informed on the subject; and therefore to suppose that the resolution to become Suttees cannot proceed so much from their having reasoned themselves into a conviction of the purity of the act itself, as from a kind of infatuation produced by the absurdities poured into their ears by ignorant brahmuns, most of whom, if asked, would be found unable to give a reason for the doctrines they inculcate. I am persuaded that *ninety-nine* out of *a hundred women* sacrifice themselves more under the influence of this infatuation than from any conviction of their own minds."* (E. Molony, Esq., Mag. Burdwan, Dec., 1818.)

"It was the prevalent opinion amongst the natives that this sacrifice would not be tolerated by the British Government."† (S. Marriott, Esq,, Tannah, Sept., 1819.)

V. Hale, Esq., Judge in the Southern Concan, (Oct., 1819,) thus shews the state of public opinion relative to the Suttee in that part of India:—"I was much gratified on finding on my arrival in this part of the Concan, that the ceremony of Suttee, at no time so commonly practised as in most parts of British India, had, *on the institution of the Hon. Company's Government entirely ceased*, apparently caused by a very general opinion which prevailed among the natives, (though certainly without reason), that the performance of this sacrifice was totally repugnant to the laws, as well as the feeling of Government; in short,—*that it would not be permitted.* This sentiment, particularly as no specific rules at that period existed for the guidance of Magistrates, and as no bad effect apparently was the result of it, I did not most certainly take the smallest pains to remove; contenting myself, in the very few instances where my permission was applied for, by neither giving nor withholding my consent, declaring, as was then literally the case, that I was ignorant whether the usage was permitted by the Government or not. The state of doubt in which these evasive answers left the minds of the applicants, I found had all the effect I could have hoped for, and in a very short time I heard no more of them: the result being that in the bounds of the late Malwan residency *not a single case of Suttee has ever occurred;* at least not in my time: and I believe I am correct when I add, neither within the four years my predecessor was stationed there; if there has it must have been performed (a very improbable circumstance) with such secrecy as to prelude the possibility of its coming to the knowledge of the local authorities."‡

One more extract may be made from the Par. Papers, (printed

* Par. Papers. p. 236. † p. 256. ‡ p. 258.—Account of YorkMeeting, p. 26.

1821), of similar import with the preceding:—"I feel emboldened, in the cause of humanity, to state, that the practice (of Suttee) *is neither prescribed by the shastra, nor encouraged by persons of education or influence.* I can speak, from positive authority, that his Highness the Rajah of Tanjore, has ever discouraged it; and I feel assured that, with the exception of a few brahmuns, who derive a nefarious reward for presiding at this infernal rite, the prohibition of the practice would give universal satisfaction."* (C. M. Lushington, Esq., Mag. at Combeconum, Sept., 1813.)

We could, with no consistency declare that to be murder to day, which we yesterday declared to be justifiable, and I do not think we ever can do so until we are armed with law opinions, that the practice of Suttees is not conformable to the Hindoo law: *and it by no means seems certain that such a construction of the law would be unattainable.*"† (W. Leycester, Esq., Chief Judge of the Nizamut Adawlut, Calcutta, May, 1821.)

"The ordinances of Menu, which are one of the principal law authorities in this part of India, do not encourage the sacrifice in the same manner as others quoted in the vivade changamana, translated by Mr. Colebrook. 'Let him not wish for death! Let him not wish for life! Let him expect his appointed time, as a hired servant expects his wages,' are doctrines more agreeable to the institutes of the oldest Hindoo legislator, who mentions doctrines very averse from self-immolation of widows; such as the raising up a son to the deceased by the widow. Here the marriage of widows is now deemed illegal, but not so in some of the most southern parts of the Peninsula. The Hindoo shastra lays down rules for securing proper provision for the widow, and confidence on the uninterrupted validity of such claims has probably proved, as a solace to their afflictions, one of the most efficacious considerations to operate to the prevention of the practice; while the persuasion which the priesthood use to widows to induce them to devote their bodies to this sacrifice, have the greatest influence on those *who, being without future protection and maintenance,* regard a future sojourn in this world with despair."‡

"I look upon this inhuman practice as one tolerated to the disgrace of the British Government; *it is ever abominated by the better sort of natives themselves, and no where is it enjoined by Hindoo law.* The authorities against self-immolation are Menu, Bhoorаspattee, and several others. The weight of authority is in favour of a rigid practice of austerities, because it is that prescribed by Menu, revered by the Hindoos as the first and greatest law of authority. *Custom* can only be legally upheld when it does not militate against *law*, '*consuetudo pro lege servator,*' will only extend to cases where no specific law exists. In the present instance there is a specific law, sanctioned by Menu, in direct opposition to authorities of inferior weight. I apprehend, the obvious absurdity of the law (exempting brahmuns from death) and the impossibility of reconciling it with our notions of justice induced its abolition. If then a *law* can be repealed from its inconsonancy with reason, the same arguments exist in a stronger de-

* Par. Papers, No. i. p. 270. † Par. Papers, No. ii. p. 68. ‡ p. 98.

gree against an inhuman, barbarous, and unjust *custom*."* (C. M. Lushington, Esq., Mag., Trichinopoly, Oct., 1819.)

The Hon. Court of Directors, in a letter addressed to the Governor General in Council, at Fort William, Bengal, dated London, June 17, 1823, thus expressed their views of the obligatory nature of Suttee, and the means of its abolition:—"Connected with the opinions expressed by many intelligent men, that *the practice of Suttee is not a tenet of religion to which the people are enthusiastically attached, but rather an abuse, fostered by interested priests and relations.* These instances of partial success do lead us to regard the notion of *prohibition*, modified according to circumstances, of this barbarous custom with rather less of apprehension than it has generally produced. Assuredly the most acceptable form of success would be that which would be brought about by such an increase of intelligence among the people as should shew them the wickedness and absurdity of the practice; next to this, we should rejoice to see the abolition effected by the influence and the co-operation of the higher order of natives."† It is gratifying to see this awfully interesting subject discussed by every class of society, and there can be no doubt that the abolition of the Suttee would be hailed in India as an act expected from the British Government, and reflecting lustre upon its administration. O may those in whose hands are the lives of thousands of hapless widows, and the destinies of millions, reflect upon the language of the Almighty:—"If thou forbear to deliver them that are drawn unto death, and those that are ready to be slain; if thou sayest, 'Behold we knew it!' doth not He that pondereth the heart consider it? and He that keepeth thy soul, doth not he know it? and shall not he render to every man according to his works." Pro. xxiv. 11, 12.

J. H. Harington, Esq., now member of Council in Calcutta, in a very interesting Minute relative to Suttees, dated Dec., 1824, thus gives his view of the fecility and safety of suppressing Suttees:—"If, as appears from the exposition of the shastra, given by the pundits of the Sudder Dewanny Adawlut, the assistance of brahmuns and others be requisite to enable the widow to devote herself in the prescribed or customary way, whether of sahamaran or anoomaran, (burning with or without the body,) it would surely be possible to prevent such aid being given by a public interdiction, with a declaration that any person hereafter causing, aiding, or in any manner promoting a female sacrifice, such as that commonly denominated a Suttee, shall be liable to a criminal prosecution, as principals or accomplices, for homicide; and that on conviction it will not be held any justification of the homicide that the person so convicted was desired by the deceased to cause, aid, or in any manner to promote her death, or that the deceased became a Suttee by a voluntary act of self-devotion. It is impossible that a legislative enactment to prevent assistance being hereafter given in the Suttee immolation, with a view to preserve the lives of a number of miserable women from suicide, in a state of affliction from the recent death of their husbands, and to put a stop to the horrible abuses and cruelties which, *unsanctioned by Hindoo laws*, have

* Par. Papers, No. ii. p. 103, 104. † Par. Papers, printed 1824, p. 45.

too frequently attended an involuntary perpetration of this sacrifice, could be imputed to any other motives than what would really govern such an enactment; and which might therefore be fairly and fully declared, without danger of its being misconstrued into any thing like a general design to put down, by authority, the religious system with which the inhuman practice referred to is imperfectly connected."*

The same Gentleman, in a paper addressed to the Right Hon. the President of the Board of Control, under date May 30, 1822, thus decidedly shews his opinion of the nature of the Suttee, and the propriety of its abolition:—"Whatever opinion may be entertained on the policy which has hitherto induced the British Government to tolerate the immolation of Hindoo widows, as considered to be in some degree a religious observance, *although it is not a prescribed duty*, as may be seen in Mr. H. Colebrook's Translation of Original Texts on the subject, (see Vol. iv. of the Transactions of the Asiatic Society), there can be no sufficient or legitimate reason for permitting a practice so repugnant to every feeling and principle of humanity, *in opposition to the only laws which can be pleaded in justification of it.*" †

The following statement is interesting, contained in a letter from T. H. Pelly, Esq., Magistrate of the Southern Concan, to the Governor in Council, Bombay, dated May 11, 1820:—"Happening to be at Penn in Dec. it was reported to me, late in the day, that a woman was about to perform the ceremony of a Suttee. Some of the respectable brahmuns were sent for, and after in vain endeavouring to persuade them from persevering in their design, they were told that if they could show *any passage* in their sacred works which went the length of *actually ordering the ceremony*, it might go on. This they said they could readily do; but could not in fact produce any thing beyond the well-known commendations bestowed on Suttees, and the equally known recapitulation of the several curious advantages derivable to the soul of the deceased by the cremation of the widow. The days were short at that season, and while these discussions were going on in the most quiet and amicable manner, the sun was rapidly sinking, and indeed nearly set. They noticed this, I imagine, and seeming unwilling to press for my sanction to an immolation, which they must have perceived I contemplated with extreme horror; they inquired if I would object to the Suttee within Angrias territory, which was close at hand. To this I replied, that I could exercise no jurisdiction there. They left me with the intention, as I conceived, of performing the ceremony beyond our line of boundary: but I found, on inquiry, that the design was abandoned altogether: and the woman is now, I believe, alive." ‡

The Magistrate of Poona, in 1823, Captain H. D. Robertson, exerted himself much for the abolition of Suttees. His discussions with the brahmuns and pundits, as given in the Parliamentary Papers, are highly interesting; an extract or two may be given.—"Chintamun Dixit, a violent man, said I had infringed their law, by saving Radabyee's life, and that had she lived they could not have permitted her to be considered in their caste. I defied him the proof of this:

* Par. Papers, No. iv. p. 10, 11. † Page 20. ‡ Page 155, 156.

and asserted the unpalatable truth that he either willfully misrepresented, or did not understand, his own law; that the shastras and commentaries upon them, by which they in those days declare themselves to be guided, precisely laid down a penance during twelve days, of no very hard description to be the terms of readmission into society of a woman who should come from the pile alive, after being once in it: and that it was positively declared to be a meritorious act, to assist in saving such a Suttee from burning."*

Addressing the natives in their language, he said:—"There is not a man in this assembly who, if he had witnessed the scene I was summoned to behold, (on Saturday, Sep. 27th), would not appreciate my present motives, and would not aid me in endeavouring to impress on the rest the propriety of some arrangement being effected, by which a repetition of it should never occur. Impressed with the conviction that the Suttee is a barbarous one; aware that *the law of your forefathers no where inculcates as a positive law or duty, the practice, but merely allows it a colour of such sanction, by such a positive endurance, that room even for doubt is left whether the sanction is not a kind of denouncement of it;* aware that your shastra, in no text, can be interpreted to attach blame or even censure to widows who do not become Suttees; that there is no slur or stain that any one may dare to throw on the character or affection of her who does not sacrifice herself; aware moreover that the present generation and yourselves attach no contempt to those who survive their partners;—you cannot but agree with me, that there exists not one good cause for not stopping the practice altogether."†

An article "*On Female Immolation,*" published in "The Friend of India," March, 1821, from which extracts were forwarded to the Hon. Court of Directors, July, 1823, and printed in the Par. Papers, July, 1825, (p. 20—26,) contains a just and powerful statement of the points at issue. The writer says:—"If it be advanced that the Hindoos think the Suttee is a religious rite, we would ask: Under what Government is the privilege of deciding on the nature of crime and punishments delegated to the subject, more especially with regard to actions which render him obnoxious to justice? If the Hindoo who burns his innocent mother brings himself to think it a religious action, are the civil authorities, to whom the preservation of her life is committed, over which life he has not even a shadow of a right, obliged to think so? Are the sacred principles of justice to be abrogated because private individuals are mistaken in their notions of the worship which is acceptable to the Deity? The admission of this principle would rend asunder the bond of society; for if the highest crime, that of murder, may go unpunished when committed under a religious pretext, what crime can we consistently punish in India? There is no species of abomination which the Hindoo code does not sanction under some shape or other. But the whole course of our judicial proceedings demonstrates that we have never acted on these principles. 'But the Hindoo law commands this murderous practice.' This we must beg leave to deny.—Menu, the parent of Indian *jurisprudence*, for

* Par. Papers, No. iv. p. 167. † page 181, 182.

whom the natives entertain such veneration, that the brahmun who possesses not a shalgram and a copy of his laws, is said to have forfeited his religious privileges:—Menu, respecting whom it is acknowledged, that 'what is contrary to his injunction is not law,' says nothing of female immolation, but on the contrary prescribes rules for the conduct of widows during the time of their natural existence. If succeeding Hindoo commentators have partially countenanced it, we would ask;—since what period have we taken those authors for our rule and guide, and substituted their precepts instead of the principles of justice? For the honour of the British character we can reply that we have never done so; we have never put to death every shoodra who has molested a brahmun by bringing an action against him for debt, robbery, or adultery. We have not cut off the hands of every shoodra who has seized a brahmun by the neck; we have not poured melted lead into the ears of every plebeian who has listened, during the last sixty years to reproaches against these twice-born favourites of heaven. Yet these injunctions, however contrary to reason, to humanity, and to the peace of mankind, are positively contained in their code. We have not therefore listened for one moment to these books, but have defended the natives from the bloody rigour of their own laws. If any one be still disposed to object, that while we have in general upheld the authority of these books, we have disannulled those laws which appeared unjust, we really know not what argument may be adduced more favourable to the abolition of female murder; for in this case it may be justly urged that if we possess a discretionary power over the Hindoo laws, the helpless widow has as strong a claim to our compassion as the members of the servile tribe, almost every individual of which is daily incurring the penalties decreed in them; and that if we make any exceptions in the execution of the Hindoo code, the unprotected female ought fully to share in them. The burning of widows is a *mere excrescence from the corrupt stock of polytheism.* We question whether *one half* of the population of India know any thing of it but by report; the number of those who feel interested in supporting it consists only of those who are personally engaged in promoting female immolation; the great majority of our native subjects are as little interested in the question as in the death of a brahmun at Cape Commerin. It does not require any great penetration to discern that those who have quietly submitted to the death of their priests when justice has demanded the sacrifice, will manifest no disquietude when in the spirit of equity and humanity, we prevent the murder of their sisters and daughters."

Charles Marsh, Esq., in the House of Commons, in 1813, thus expressed himself relative to the obligatory nature of Suttees:—"*It is enjoined by no positive precept of the Hindoo religion.* It is a species of overstrained interpretation of its duties: and the offspring of that fanaticism which will inevitably grow up, and has more or less grown up, under every system of religion."* Ought not such fanaticism to be corrected?

The late C. Grant, Esq., in his "Observations on the Manners of

* Dr. John's Pamphlet on the Suttee, p. 96.

the Natives of British India," adverts to this custom, and intimates, that to say we should continue to allow of these great disorders in "all time to come" would be "too daring a conclusion."*

The philanthropic and eloquent Wilberforce thus pleaded the cause of benighted India, in the British Senate, in 1813.—"Oh Sir, if we lived nearer these unfortunate people, their distressed situation would exact from us more prompt relief. It was formerly my task to plead the cause of a people whose woes affected every heart, who were finally rescued from the situation in which they groaned by the abolition of the Slave Trade. That cause was doubtless the cause of suffering humanity; but I declare that, even if we exclude the consideration of religion; *humanity appears to me to be still more concerned in the cause I am now pleading than in that of which I was formerly the advocate.*"

The Rev. T. Scott of Aston Sandford, in his valuable Commentary, has the following remarks on Numbers xxxv. 33:—"So ye shall not pollute the land wherein ye are: for blood it defileth the land: and the land cannot be cleansed of the blood that is shed therein but by the blood of him that shed it." "The *connivance* of our Government in the burning of widows, and in human sacrifices, and in other species of murder committed in our East Indian dominions, under the pretext of an idolatrous religion, is wholly unjustifiable, and *burdens our land, and all connected with those distant regions*, with the guilt of blood *not expiated by that of those who shed it.*"—The blood of Suttees cry to Britain. O may she soon "make inquisition for blood," that "the blood of the souls of the poor innocents" may not be "found upon her skirts."

It appears very important to ascertain the judgment of the Hindoos themselves upon the obligation of the rite of Suttee. In the Bewasta, received from Mutoonjoy Pundit of the Supreme Court in 1817, respecting the burning of Hindoo widows and other sacrifices among the Hindoos, Menu is not mentioned among the various authorities quoted; and it is acknowledged "on the subject of anoogumum the shastras exhibit a great variety of opinions; but no difference prevails with regard to the propriety of leading a life of austerity."

Ram Mohunroy in 1818 published in Calcutta, in Bengalee and English, a pamphlet entitled, "A Conference between an Advocate and an Opponent of the practice of burning widows," which I should be happy to see reprinted in this country. A quotation or two from it will shew the sentiments of the humane and enlightened among the Hindoos relative to the Suttee:—"The Veda declares—'By living in the practice of regular and occasional duties the mind may be purified. By hearing and reflecting and constantly meditating on the Supreme Being, absorption in Brumhu may be attained. Therefore from a desire during life, of future fruition, life ought not to be destroyed!' Menu, Yagnyuvulkyu, and others, have, in their respective codes of law, prescribed to widows the duties of ascetics only. The ancient saints and holy teachers and their commentators and yourselves, (addressing Advocates of the Suttee,) as well as we, and all others, agree

* Townley's Answer to the Abbe Dubois, p. 189.

that Menu is better acquainted than any other lawgivers with the spirit of the Vedas. He has directed widows to spend their lives as ascetics." It is thus closed:—"It is to me a source of great satisfaction that you (the Advocates) are now ready to take this matter into your serious consideration. By forsaking prejudice and reflecting on the shastra, what is really conformable to its precepts may be perceived, and the *evil and disgrace brought on this community, by the crime of female murder, will cease.*"

Mr. Townley, in his "Answer to the Abbe Dubois," shews the opinions of the Hindoos upon this subject:—"I have heard of the reply being repeatedly given to the expostulations of Europeans; "*If there is any blame in our proceedings, it belongs to you yourselves, for we are acting under British sanction.*" He adds, "The native who instructed me in the Bengalee language, (who was a brahmun of more than ordinary intelligence,) frequently expressed his surprize to me that Government did not issue an order that no more Suttees should be permitted, intimating his conviction that no commotion whatever would ensue." *

Ah why is Britain afraid to do justice upon those who shed innocent blood?—"Where are the bowels of our mercy?—Where our fears of the retributive justice of Heaven?—How long shall this scourge continue to desolate India, and dishonour Britain? We may answer in the memorable language of a brahmun, '*Till the British Government shall think proper to abolish it.*'" †

"The pundits have intimated that if Government will pass a regulation, amercing by fine every brahmun who attends a burning, or every zemindar who permits him to attend it, the practice cannot long continue. The ceremony, unsanctified by the presence of the priests, will lose its dignity in the eyes of the people." (Southey.)

When Dr. Johns was in India (in 1812) the principal brahmuns at the Mission Press, Serampore, were asked, whether the interference of the Government to suppress so horrid a custom would be objected to by the natives. They promptly answered *that it would not*, and encouraged the idea of such an interference." ‡

"It ought to be considered, that some of the most respectable pundits do not approve the practice, and would be happy if it were abolished: while many others *reproach us for permitting it to exist.*" §

In the Asiatic Journal for July, 1826, published in London, are three letters in English, written by Bengalees, on the subject of Suttees, which are very curious compositions, and show the sentiments of sensible natives on the nature of this appalling rite. We can give but a short extract or two.—"Her brother Roopnarain Gosaul, who is supposed to be a wealthy man, and being so long in the Hon. Company's service, ought to be discharged from his place, and prosecuted in the Supreme Court for giving countenance to such an inhuman act. *No body anger could be minded when a life is concerned; she ought to be prevented to burn.* If Governor General gives orders to remove

* Townley's Answer to the Abbe Dubois, p. 180. 190. † "Grimshawe's Appeal," p. 24. ‡ See Dr. John's Pamphlet, p. 92. Account of York Meeting, p. 23, 24. § Asiatic Observer, No. 8. Oct., 1824, p. 371.

the woman from her relations, at her pronouncing that she will burn, and allow her to remain *one day* in a comfortable place with English Ladies that understands the country's language, there is no doubt her mind shall be purified, and her foolish thoughts shall be removed, and will not be anxious to do such a base act as to burn with dead person." (Muddunmohun Mullick, Calcutta, Jan. 27, 1826.)

"I fully agree with the sentiments contained in Muddunmohun's letter. If the Government in Council gives order to remove all the women on pronouncing that they will burn, to be placed with an intelligent English person to persuade them to the contrary, and not allow any of the relations to converse, or make them take *intoxicated drugs*, they will never die in such an inhuman manner. I have lost my wife these *six years*, and have not married again for fear she may burn with my body at my death.—The Hindoo woman have no sense; they hear from their superiors the cremation is an holy act, and they are fool enough to listen it, which only induce them to express their sentiments that they will burn; and as soon as such a declaration is obtained all the unfeeling relations uses all their exertions to induce the poor unfortunate widows to suffer such a cruel death. I hope you will not refuse to have this appeared in your interesting Paper, and oblige me." (Sunchurn Sill, Calcutta, Jan. 31, 1826.)

What shall urge British humanity, magnanimity, and justice, to abolish, without delay, the bloody rite of Suttee? *Let the magnitude of the evil be seriously considered.* The following is an account of the number of Suttees under the Presidencies of Bengal, Madras, and Bombay, during the years specified.—

SUTTEES IN THE BENGAL PRESIDENCY.								
1815	1816	1817	1818	1819	1820	1821	1822	1823
378	442	707	839	650	597	654	583	575
MADRAS PRESIDENCY.								
1817 *to* 1819, 183,—*Average per annum* 61. *No returns since.*								
BOMBAY PRESIDENCY.*								
	1819	1820	1821	1822	1823			
	42	67	50	48	38			

The aggregate af these details is 5853. "What a tragic history would a complete detail of these burnings make!" Could they have been assembled in one city (say Calcutta) for a general massacre, would they have perished? No!—but is the evil, the guilt, the responsibility, less because these fires are lighted up daily and in various parts of the land? "The question (discussed here) is *a question of life or of death*, and consequently we must bring to the consideration of it all those rules of evidence, and all that process of argument, which can alone satisfy men's sober judgment, and direct them in a decision, which is to terminate either in the death-warrant of the vic-

* See Par. Papers, Nos. 1, 2, 3, 4.—Account of York Meeting, p. 21.

tims or in the revocation of their degraded and mournful lot." Britain delays to speak the decisive word that shall save thousands of unhappy widows from death, but, "*On whom will the blood of the many thousand victims that are destined to perish be visited?* This is a solemn and momentous question, before which we may well pause and weigh all the present and all the future consequences. It cannot be dissembled, that the charge of guilt attaches primarily to the *Government of India*, who are the conscious spectators of the act, and largely possessing the means, are yet deterred from employing those means for its suppression. It next attaches to the *British Government* at home, who acquiesce in the motives that influence this reluctance. And finally, the *whole British people become parties to this moral guilt*, if knowing, as they do, the existence of the crime, they do not consider themselves pledged to use all lawful means for abolishing a rite, derogatory to the British character, forming an anamoly in the administration of civil law, and involving a flagrant breach of the law of God."*

The Marquis of Hastings would have "abolished the atrocious practice, if he could have relied upon the popular feeling being in his favour in our own country, and that the danger was felt not in India, (Proh dolor!) but only in England."† Let the inhabitants of Great Britain and Ireland speak and supplicate that no more innocent blood may be shed. Bedford, in 1823, and the village of Crail, near Edinburgh, in 1825, have taken the lead in this work of justice and mercy. The present year, 1827, is likely to see something important done. The abolition of human sacrifices has been discussed in the Court of East India Proprietors, and advances made towards the attainment of this desired object. Notice is given in the House of Commons of a motion on the subject of Suttees, for May 24th, and petitions have been sent from York, Rochdale, Colchester, &c. and others are preparing at Derby, Loughborough, Retford, &c. The most concise and comprehensive form of a petition I have seen, is that of Loughborough, which is as follows:—"To the Honourable the Commons of the United Kingdom of Great Britain and Ireland, in Parliament assembled.

"The humble Petition of the Inhabitants of the Town of ——— and its Vicinity,

"Sheweth,—That your Petitioners learn with extreme concern that the inhuman and impious practice in India, of burning Widows on the funeral pile of their husbands, still continues.

"That your Petitioners while they gratefully acknowledge that of late years exertions have been made for the moral and religious improvement of India, and that the influence of the British Government has been successfully exerted in the prevention of many superstitious cruelties hitherto practised by the Natives; would earnestly implore your Honourable House to command such further exercise of authority as may secure the abrogation of the practice, so opposed to the law of God, and so revolting to humanity. And your Petitioners will ever pray."

Under the law of Moses even uncertain murder was to be expi-

* Grimshawe's Appeal, p. 20. 26. † Account of York Meeting, p. 6.

ated, and the people taught to pray;—"Be merciful, O Lord, unto thy people Israel, whom thou hast redeemed, and lay not innocent blood unto thy people of Israel's charge." (Deu. xxi. 8.) May Britain feel her responsibility to "put away the guilt of innocent blood."

> "Ye British matrons, husbands, sires,
> Your souls with soft compassion glowing;
> O haste to quench the horrid fires
> Whence human blood is sadly flowing;
> *With your lov'd King and Country plead,*
> *Implore the Senate of your nation*
> *That British India may be freed*
> *From scenes of such abomination.*"

The existence of Suttees and other cruel rites in India, for many ages, is a proof of its benighted, degraded state. Bible and Missionary Societies are the great means of promoting its conversion to Christianity. "The Gospel is the power of God to salvation to every one that believeth." I have seen a Bengalee Christian and a preacher who, when a boy, set fire to the pile that consumed his mother to ashes. Behold the triumph of Christianity!—Let the friends of humanity and of true religion prosecute the good work of evangelizing India and the East, for their "labour is not in vain in the Lord."

We shall close in the impressive language of a Writer in the Asiatic Observer, No. viii. (published in Calcutta, Oct. 1824). Speaking of this cruel practice, it is observed:—"How many noble souls have ventured on some bold enterprize, without seeing how they could accomplish their design; yet, by close attention and perseverence, a way his opened to their view, and means have offered themselves almost spontaneously for forwarding their wishes, so that at length they have attained to that which at first appeared to them almost impossible to be acquired. Indeed the noblest plans and institutions by which our country (Britain) is adorned, and our happiness increased, have originated in this manner. Let *one man of influence in society* take the object into consideration, deliberately, and with a determination to find out some plan to which he can solicit the attention of the public, and we have as little doubt of his success as we have of the disposition of the public to assist him. Various ideas have been started on this subject and some of them, were they adopted, might prove beneficial. It has been thought that it would be good for the inhabitants of Calcutta to present a petition to the Supreme Government here, or through them to *our own Legislators at home.* It would certainly be an honourable thing to those who made it, and entitle them to a place among the friends of India to the latest age. It has been suggested that it would be very honourable to the ladies in Calcutta were they all to unite in presenting a petition and soliciting the Lady of the Governor General to do them the honour of putting her name first. This would display the humanity and sympathy of the Calcutta ladies, and have a great practical effect, by leading many to impress on their husbands the importance of rescuing a degraded part of the female sex. If all *the Knights* of the present day could be persuaded to undertake the rescuing of Bengalee widows from the flames, they would attempt a nobler deed than was ever achieved since the order was instituted; and, should they be successful, would transmit to posterity a name more honourable than any or all of their brethren. Another plan that has been proposed, and acted upon in part, is, that Houses of Agency, Mercantile Houses, &c., would set their faces against this practice, by dismissing from their employment any person who has been brutal enough *to burn his own mother*. This would teach the natives in general the abhorrence that Europeans have of the crime, and would, in many instances, prevent it from being committed."

"We are encouraged, from the spirit of the British Nation, and from the prophecies of Scripture, confidently to anticipate an end to the miseries we now deplore. That a Parliament which has abolished the Slave Trade, will for ever permit the burning of widows, we can never believe. Slavery did not receive its death-blow at once: many blows were aimed at the monster before its head was broken; and its carcase is not even yet all consumed. So it may be in the case under discussion: it may be brought forward several times before all objections to it, real and fictitious, are answered; but, notwithstanding this, *unless humanity and wisdom perish from the British Senate, we are certain that sooner or later they will put an end to this horrid practice.* We argue, not from the cessation of many cruel ceremonies among other nations that this will certainly be the case; we have a surer word of prophecy on which to depend: the MOST HIGH has declared that he will give his SON "the heathen for his inheritance, and the uttermost parts of the earth for his possession." If these nations are given to him, whose law is love, and whose Gospel is peace, then will be brought to pass the saying that is written: "The wolf and the lamb shall feed together, and the lion shall eat straw like the bullock; and dust shall be the serpent's meat. They shall not hurt nor destroy in all my holy mountain, saith the Lord."*

* Asiatic Observer, p. 369, 370, 374, 375.

THE END.

CONTENTS.